This book if borrowed by a friend,
Right welcome shall he be,
To read, to study,
...not to lend,
But to return to me

Not that imparted knowledge doth
Diminish learnings store
But books I find if often lent,
Return to me no more.

Ginny Kenreich

*With his own hands he had put the flames to his
own house, the richest on the island. With it he
destroyed all the wealth he had accumulated during
the period of Toussaint's ascendency, making himself homeless.*

BLACK MAJESTY

THE LIFE OF CHRISTOPHE
KING OF HAITI

BY

JOHN W. VANDERCOOK

WITH DRAWINGS BY
MAHLON BLAINE

HARPER & BROTHERS PUBLISHERS
NEW YORK AND LONDON
MCMXXVIII

FIRST PRINTING, FEBRUARY, 1928
SECOND PRINTING, FEBRUARY, 1928
THIRD PRINTING, MARCH, 1928
FOURTH PRINTING, MARCH, 1928
FIFTH PRINTING, MAY, 1928
SIXTH PRINTING, JUNE, 1928
SEVENTH PRINTING, JULY, 1928
EIGHTH PRINTING, AUGUST, 1928
NINTH PRINTING, SEPTEMBER, 1928

TO MARGARET

FOREWORD

THIS is the life of a man. I have added nothing to the sparse records of old books and the fading memories that linger in the minds of men in his own country. Nor have I left anything out, except a few foolish, though extraordinarily common, legends that I found had no historical basis whatever. Christophe, as is often the ill-fortune of great men, has been remembered chiefly by his enemies and the cruel and silly tales they told of him.

This is not a "work of reference," but I have appended a selected bibliography.

LIST OF ILLUSTRATIONS
BY MAHLON BLAINE

[ix]

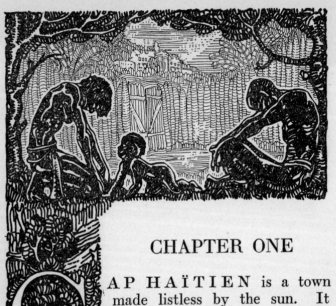

CHAPTER ONE

CAP HAÏTIEN is a town made listless by the sun. It sprawls along the edge of a shallow bay on the north coast of the island of Haiti 800 miles southeast of Florida. The streets are narrow and either swarming and noisy with negro men and women or utterly quiet but for the dull droning of flies in the gutters. Low houses flank the roads with not an inch to spare. Sometimes one comes upon a building freshly kalsomined rose-red, or yellow, or pale blue, but on most green mold has etched drab patterns in plaster rotted by long neglect.

Life for the blacks of the Cap is easy. The eternal warmth of summer, a few plantains, yams, loud laughter and the swift crackle of patois talk in the markets suffice for a barefoot citizenry.

Behind the city is a vast plain that lies between two mountain ranges. Mangrove and dwarf scrub forest make of it a desolate, warm wilderness. Along a muddy road eastward from the Cap there are huddled groups of shacks thatched with palm branches and wattled with reeds. Filth-caked swine, starved curs, and naked negro babies fraternize on the hard-packed earth. Dulleyed old men and tempestuous black wenches laze and shrill and talk the days away. Sometimes an old woman piles wild produce—a few sticks of red logwood, a bunch of green plantains, or a dozen stalks of sugar cane—on the back of a donkey and rides in to the public market at the Cap. She sells her stuff and in the late twilight rides home again with a few purchases made in the town. The scene never varies. It has scarcely changed during four generations while the black peasants of Haiti have slipped ever deeper into stupor and dirt and dreamlessness.

Black Majesty

But once, over a hundred years ago, a great king made Cap Haïtien his capital. He was a black man who was born a slave, but under him the city of the Cap and the country round about presented a different picture.

There was a theater in the Cap and there were schools. No one was indolent or dirty, for indolence and filth were forbidden by the King. Factories were busy and the bay was filled with ships. The great plain between the hills was a sugar field, the finest in the world, its area measured by hundreds of square miles. Along the roads out of the town, roads bedded evenly with gleaming white stones, were plantations owned by negroes who bore with dignity the titles of duke and baron and count. The northern half of Haiti was a kingdom that during its brief span of life ranked in the opinion of Europe with the most forceful of the New World powers. There were two men of transcendent greatness then— Napoleon of France and the King of Haiti, Henry Christophe, the only man alive who had defeated him in war.

In Haiti now only a few remember King Christophe's name. But he foresaw this, and while he lived raised a monument more permanent than the name of a king, when that name

·[3]·

is left to slip to sure oblivion over the loose, full lips of sullen black men of an island in the tropic sea.

Mariners who come into the harbor of Cap Haïtien take bearings on clear days on the Citadel of Christophe. It is a fortress that even from the sea twenty miles away looms in majestic silhouette against the sky. It squares off the peak of a mountain that lifts above the hills that neighbor it. They are shouldering hills, covered with thick jungle and littered with masses of titanic stone. But Christophe's Citadel masters them, broods over them in its loneliness, its isolation, and its achievement of the sense of the sure supremacy of human greatness.

The Citadel, "La Ferrière"—The Blacksmith's Pouch,—as it was called in Christophe's time, has been empty and deserted ever since an October night one hundred and seven years ago, when the great King died. It is a fortress larger and more massive than the Tower of London, yet it straddles a mountain peak three thousand feet above the sea. It is the most impressive structure ever conceived by a negro's brain or executed by black hands in all the world in all the tens of thousands of years of the race's history.

The end of the Citadel which thrusts toward

the sea is built like the prow of a ship, a prow that rises a hundred and thirty feet from the crest of a slope so steep men and donkeys must climb in three-quarters of a circle to reach the base of the wall. Behind it, in a central weed-grown court sheltered on all sides by the ramparts, is a crude, small shed of stone with a peaked roof. It stands less than shoulder high and there is no marking to save its drab simplicity. At one end is an opening no larger than the entrance to a dog-house and within is a pile of broken stones mixed with disintegrated mortar. Under the litter lies all that remains, after the lapse of a forgetful century, of the body of the King. It is his tomb. . . . At night the bats that hang in clusters in the dark dungeons underground come out and swerve eerily under the pale moon over it. At twilight, when the evening mists lift up from the sea they break against the prow of the Citadel so that to the black peasants who watch from the valleys the silent fortress seems to move and be riding with the impetus of a wind into the shadowing skies.

No one knows where King Christophe was born.

In after years the King himself was curiously reticent upon the point. Apparently he had two answers ready. A Royal Almanac prepared by a courtier and published at the presses at the King's Palace of Sans Souci gives the date of his birth as October 6, 1767, and his birthplace as Grenada, that mountainous West Indian island of the Windward group not far north of Trinidad. But old men who still live in Haiti, whose grandfathers were numbered among the friends and councilors of the King, say he came from Kitts, a tinier, nearer British island, which in the King's time still went by its old name of St. Christopher.

His name, Henry Christophe, piles up considerable evidence for the St. Kitts party. The Henry, spelled always with the English "y," and "Christophe" after St. Christopher, of course . . . so they argue.

His birth, wherever it occurred, surely had nothing of note to mark it. A planter in those days kept no record of the advent of chattels so cheap as black slave babies. A note, no doubt, was made in the plantation inventory and perhaps the white master found a moment to go down to the slave compound to reward the mother with a silver coin and the admonition to bear more strong male babies as often as possible. Then surely he breathed deep to get the stench of the sweating slave-corrals out of his nostrils and promptly forgot Henry Christophe.

History has no information to offer concerning this planter on whose lands Christophe was born, except that he was a Frenchman, although a resident of a British island. Half a century later his daughter, then fatherless and fallen in fortunes, was an honored guest at the King's Palace of Sans Souci . . . and had great difficulty at first in learning to address Henry by his full titles.

Nor is anything known of Christophe's father and mother except that they were negro slaves brought from West Africa across the Middle Passage to work the fields of the island, Grenada or Kitts, whichever it was. If, however, one may guess safely from the one extant portrait of the King, his ancestry derived from the people of the hot plains of the Soudan where the aristocrats of Africa are found. He was, like them, very tall, straight-featured as a Roman and supremely proud.

Of Christophe's childhood we know all there is to know. Like all slave children of the sugar lands, he was disregarded by black and white society alike. First he spent a year straddled helpless athwart his mother's naked hip in a sling of cloth tied over her left shoulder. Then came another year of sitting forgotten with other black, brown, and yellow babies in the hot sand by the slaves' mud shacks, wailing now and then at the sting of ants and burrowing chigoes. And childhood after that . . . one long, gallant summertime when a black was free, free for the only time till death, and justly for that long season, more free than any white child ever was.

From dawn, when the sun came like a carnival, flinging arches of rainbow over the island mountain peaks, until it dipped again across the world into the sunset sea, there was nothing for young Henry and the other children of the compound to do but play down the weedy lanes between the shabby plantain trees and suck short, sticky lengths of sugar cane.

On the great plantations there were scenes of glamor. The great, grinding rolls of the macerator at the sugar mill, the odorous rum vats, the iron half-sphere pans of steaming molasses over charcoal fires watched by slaves the same rich sable brown as the brew they tended, must have seemed worth endless hours of watching. The black children must have wondered at a state of things that set the master and his family so curiously apart from the world of toiling men and women whose skin was dark. Surely Christophe wondered. No one not born with too long a heritage of weariness could have helped but marvel at the white house behind the screen of pepper trees, where no one ever worked or sweated, where no one ever wept or felt the whip-lash—or, for the matter of that, ever laughed.

There were the long warm days, the slow shimmer of heat mirage over the compound yard and the pallid green of the endless, drowsing cane fields; an everlasting noonday babyhood for the slaves' black children, for Christophe, destined to be king.

He had no school, no teaching and no family, except the nondescript slave family and the mother too weary for much but a tired embrace of passion at the day's end before the moon climbed among the pricking stars and sleep came

gratefully to claim Africa's lost children . . . a
puzzled, senseless childhood for a king.

Then the day came when the planter decided
that Christophe, now nearly seven, was old
enough to earn his keep. He apprenticed him
to the negro who followed the trade of mason on
the place. Christophe's childhood ended.

If one is to judge by the fortress on the mountain peak, during the five years he carried stones
and mixed mortar he learned the job of mason
very well. Then, when he was twelve, he ran
away. A French sailing master gave him refuge.

The ship sailed northwest to Saint Domingue,
as Haiti was then called, and put in at the harbor
of Cap François, later known as Cap Haïtien.

The island at that time, particularly the western half of it owned by France, was considered
the most valuable overseas possession of any
European power. For many years the slavers
who plied their trade between the Guinea Coast
and the West Indies had made it a point to save
the pick of their cargoes for Cap François.
There, more than at any other New World port,
the planters could afford to pay top prices for
black flesh. The captain anticipated a neat profit.

It was in the month of August, 1779, when
he reached his destination and let his yard-arms

rattle to the deck in the haven of the bay. He found the roadstead filled with ships.

M. le Comte d'Estaing, admiral of a squadron of the navy of the King of France and a former governor of Saint Domingue, had put into the harbor of Cap François just before him with twenty-four ships of the line. He had announced that, as a result of a visit to the king of one Benjamin Franklin, the colony of Saint Domingue had been put under contribution to supply 1,500 men to go to the immediate assistance of the colonies on the American mainland.

Tables had been set up under awnings on populous street corners and young officers, perspiring and impatient in their bright uniforms, were setting down the names of those who stood in line to volunteer.

It was a poor time to sell a slave, but the captain who had brought Christophe to Saint Domingue was lucky. He chanced upon a young French naval officer who wanted a boy to oil his knee-boots and serve him at mess. The deal was quickly concluded and Henry set out to sea again.

The French fleet sailed past the rocky promontory that guards Cap François harbor from the open sea and set its course due north for the United States.

With full sails set and the banners of the king at mastheads, it made a worthy spectacle in the yellow glare of a tropic afternoon. Fifteen hundred and fifty men of Saint Domingue, blacks and mulattoes and whites, sailed with 2,200 fellow-volunteers from Guadeloupe and Martinique. All the town came down to the waterside to see them off.

Lovely ladies of France, resplendent in their jewels and laces and full skirts of rich stuffs from Europe, sat in the carriages which lined the waterfront. The artisans and shopkeepers, good stolid citizens of French communes who took none too kindly to a voluntary exile of perpetual sunshine, put up their shutters for the afternoon and mingled with the gentry to watch the sails against the sky. Behind the rank of whites came the dapper free mulattoes, straight-featured, scornful, standing apart from the blacks by choice, away from the whites by strict unwritten law. Behind them all, filling the ways between the white and yellow houses that led back through the town away from the harbor front, massed the blacks, a voiceless, craning, amorphous mob, full-mouthed, strong-bodied, sweating from the crowding and the heat. It was a last rich pageant of a time and society destined never to foregather again for so impersonal a show. . .

Aboard one of the ships setting out to sea stood a twelve-year-old black boy, nicknamed Christophe—later to be a king.

On a jetty, his bare feet hanging in the dirty wash of sea against the piles, sat a stalwart young negro who had been brought not long since from Africa in manacles in the hold of a slave-ship. This was Jean Jacques Dessalines. There was nothing to mark him as different from a thousand others like him in the crowd, except, perhaps, that his squat ugliness, his bullet head, his gross black lips, and his beady, piercing eyes might have demanded an unwilling second glance. Certainly few in all the city were further down on the scale of things. He'd brought a good price, but because of his ugliness, an ugliness that gave warning of a stubborn, violent character, the buyers for the white planters had let him go to a negro, a disgrace and an ill-fortune for any slave. . . . As yet he had scarcely mastered French, the language of his forcibly adopted country. It was

still by no means easy for him to pronounce his
own name—Jean Jacques Dessalines—conferred
upon him by his master. . . . On that long-ago
August afternoon surely he had no inkling of
the curious destiny that was to write that sonorous name across the sky as emperor. He was
content to watch the ships of Comte d'Estaing
slipping down the world beyond the hazy line
where sea met sky and to ponder in his dark
young mind the cause of things and the hatred
already born for the laughing whites in the carriages on Waterside.

The stage was set, though none of the leading
actors had yet learned his part. Young Christophe, bound overseas for his first taste of war,
surly black Dessalines idling in dirty rags, and,
seated on the coachman's box of a carriage that
had driven in that day from an outlying plantation, a little negro, already middle-aged, named
François Dominique Toussaint, in later years
called L'Ouverture, "The Opener," the "First of
the Blacks," the greatest soldier of his race, the
destroyer of Napoleon's hopes for a colonial empire, and the father of negro liberty in the New
World.

The fleet passed out of sight in the gathering
twilight. Young Christophe ate his soldier's

·[14]·

rations on the rolling wooden deck, Dessalines
shuffled barefoot through the town, and Toussaint turned his horses' heads toward home.
Saint Domingue, France's richest, fairest colony,
could sleep through untroubled nights for many
years to come.

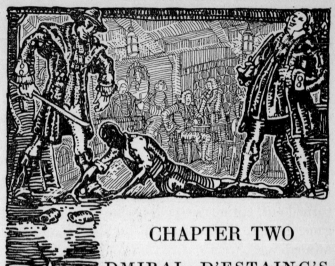

CHAPTER TWO

ADMIRAL D'ESTAING'S warships reached the mouth of the Savannah River on the coast of Georgia, swayed at anchor through a month of rain, and then, rather ridiculously, sailed south again. The expedition had been wholly futile—except in the effect it had upon one negro child.

When Henry Christophe returned to Saint Domingue he carried with him vivid, troubling recollections. He had seen tall blacks from Martinique, slender young mulattoes of Saint Domingue, grizzled soldiers of France, and lean-faced farmers of this new United States die with

queer fraternity for a thing he'd never heard of:
liberty, they called it, and the war a revolution.

A mulatto volunteer with the eyes and chin of
a poet, a youth named Chavannes, had told him
something of the cause they fought for—and had
talked with fierce intensity of a half-formed
dream of liberty at home.

The ships bearing the Saint Domingan volunteers reached Cap François. Again the town
turned out, but not so gayly. Nor did those who
came down to the waterfront stay long from their
affairs.

The volunteers made their landing, got their
pay, and went to their homes. When the last
small boats had beached a few in the crowd found
their men had fallen in the strangers' war at a
siege that still continued. Henry's master, who
was going home to France and had no further
use for a black servant boy, sold him to a free
negro at the Cap, an innkeeper named Coidovic,
proprietor of the Hôtel de la Couronne.

Coidovic wanted neither a stonemason's ap-
prentice nor an officer's body servant, but the
stables needed another hand. Christophe became a stable-boy and time and events slowed
down for him.

If one may judge by the fine taste of horse-

flesh which he displayed later on when he had
his own stables at Sans Souci, he took not un-
kindly to the trade of groom. His duties were
simple. All inns of the time kept a black boy
outside the door to take the bridles tossed him
by guests who came in from the plantations or
from the military barracks outside of town. If
the customer indicated that he expected to stay
for more than a glass, Christophe would find
stable room and fodder for his horse in the open
shed in the courtyard behind the inn. . . . But
there were endless drowsy hours of tropic afternoon when no guests appeared and there was
nothing for the serious, slender little boy to do
but listen to the hum of the flies and snatch illegal
naps in the shuttered gloom of the café bar.

In a few years Coidovic raised Christophe to
the position of waiter and billiard marker. It
was a job any slave might envy. Apart from its
pleasant and not very strenuous duties, it carried
with it a chance of that unheard-of thing for
those times, money in pocket, put there by generous gentlemen whose taste for rum and gam-
bling made them contemptuous of small change.

Evidently Christophe was popular both with
the guests of the café and with Coidovic, for by
the time he'd reached his early twenties he had

saved enough to buy his freedom. This was a change of status made possible for a negro slave of Saint Domingue only by having at the same time an indulgent master and a full purse.

The Hôtel de la Couronne was patronized by the better class of whites, and of course they talked of their problems. Nor did they trouble to lower their voices so a young black waiter with a tray would not overhear. They talked of their negro mistresses and of the comely mulatto whores who supplied Cap François with whatever its quiet, oppressive nights had of glamour, passion and forgetful laughter. And they talked with cruel and fretful contempt of the children of these women who, a tradition of an earlier, less jealous time had ruled, must be freed by their fathers.

The class composed of these children and their descendants had grown too large and the whites had grown vindictive.

Saint Domingue, when one came to think of it, was a nervous sort of place. There were 40,000 whites, their number split in sharp division

between planters and the class composed of artisans and traders, 24,000 free mulattoes, 500,000
slaves; certainly a very powder-barrel of a colony for all its wealth and ease and surface
brilliancy.

Each class hated all the others. The guests
of the café joked about it, finding comfort in
voicing private worries in the carefree surround-
ings of a wineshop. They thought of new ways
of showing their contempt for those less than
human cattle whose hair had a reprehensible urge
to curl.

The mulatto freedmen, the *affranchis,* were
their particular absorption. They were technically as free as the whitest Frenchman, but the
whites, urged on by the jealousy of wives who
found it difficult in the enervation of the tropics
to compete with the robust charms of negro
women, sought every way to make them feel the
inferiority of the black taint. Mulatto soldiers
of the colonial militia wore a uniform of a different cut and color from that worn by similar regiments of white men. Even the mulatto planters,
many of whom were as rich and as proud as their
blond neighbors, were forbidden to wear certain
desirable colors and textiles favored by the fash-

ion of the time. They sat apart at church and at the play.

The common truth was that they were, as a rule, severer masters to their black slaves and therefore even more fiercely loathed and feared by them. This was something in their favor, the whites admitted. It was comforting, said the French, to think that the two classes would never agree for rebellion.

Christophe overheard and pondered. Once, just once, he dared put in a word of his own.

A rich planter and an officer from the barracks were playing billiards one night. Christophe was marking their scores. A point, forgotten more than a hundred years ago, came up in their talk on which they differed. Soon the two gentlemen, neither of whom was much the wiser for his wine, began to quarrel. Christophe interrupted to say the officer was right. Whereupon the planter spun around and slapped young Henry on the mouth. . . .

That is all there is to the story—except that twenty-five years later when King Henry ruled from his Palace of Sans Souci, he learned that the planter was still living in the town. It was a strange twist of fate that this man among all others had survived the terrible years that inter-

vened. But the King and Fate were partners.
One night when the palace was asleep Christophe
put on his sword and walked twenty miles alone
down the Royal Road into the silent city. He
found a door and knocked. A head appeared at
a window and he called the old man down. He
reminded him of that quarrel long ago and of
the slave he had struck across the mouth. Then
they fought in the empty road and when the
King had killed his enemy in fair fight he went
back through the quiet dawn to his palace.

The Bastille fell in 1789 and the news lit the
fuse of the powder-barrel colony of Saint Domingue. No one was contented. Even the whites
wanted a change. They saw in the sudden blazing of the revolutionary mood a long-craved opportunity to get rid of the governor-general and
the autocratic powers he held from the toppling
King of France. They elected a colonial assembly and wrote a constitution that cut the colony
almost wholly free from the domination of the
mother country. In France representatives of
the free mulattoes knew their chance had come.

The echo of the passions that were stirring Europe swelled the murmurous mood of even the blacks in the corrals that lay scattered over the warm hillsides. But the time was not yet ripe for them.

A year passed. Young Christophe, his straight-featured face expressionless save for the fire in eyes of exceptional size, wore a starched white shirt, carried a little tray of clinking glasses, and listened to the café talk. Word came that the National Assembly in Paris had granted the right of taking part in the election of the colonial assembly to all freemen irrespective of their color. The murmur grew to a sullen roar.

News soon found its way to the billiard room of the Crown Hotel. A white man in the southern part of the island had been dragged from his house and beheaded by a mob for daring to suggest that the mulattoes be favored. A seventy-year-old *affranchi* had been tied to the tail of a horse and dragged through the streets as an "example." Mobs of infuriated whites all over the island were burning the sugar refineries of yellow men who had made the insolent mistake of growing rich. Christophe heard—and marked the billiard shots of the men who still found leisure for a game or two.

Soon Cap François turned out for another holiday. The tradespeople put up their shutters. In the early afternoon the streets were filled with crowding men and women bound for the waterfront to witness an uglier show than the town had seen for many years. Two mulattoes were to be smashed on a wooden rack and then tied to a wheel in full view of the mob and peering sun—"To stay as long as it would please God to preserve their lives," so the indictment read.

A great number of the rich planters were there, besides the members of the Northern Provincial Assembly, who attended in full state regalia— but they did not look toward the place in the middle of the square where the crack of bones under the executioner's iron rod and the unwilling gasps of the dying men turned other ears and eyes. The whites watched the mulattoes who stood in silent little groups in the shelter of the house walls at the edge of the square. This show was being staged for them and it was important that they understand. The short, stout quadroon upon the rack, whose weak mouth let forth such piteous cries of pain, was Ogé, the man the *affranchis* had sent to France to represent them at the National Assembly. He had come back to Saint Domingue and dared demand the rights

·[24]·

They did not look toward the place in the middle of the square where the crack of bones under the executioner's iron rod and the unwilling gasps of the dying men turned other ears and eyes.

of his class. And the man dying beside him was his friend Chavannes, whom Christophe had known at Savannah. His crime had been that he had sheltered Ogé and that he had fled with him after the defeat of the tiny army they had gathered to defend their persons and their cause.

Young Christophe, in his starched white shirt and waiter's apron, stood in the crowd and watched. He remembered the youth who had whispered in the light of the swaying ships' lamps in the night mists of Savannah, who had dreamed so bravely of a future in which he would play a gallant part.

Ogé and Chavannes died bravely.

In the procession that filed in silence after the executioner who rode through the gathering twilight to put up the dead men's heads on poles beside the road, walked an ugly little old coachman named Toussaint and a hulking black man, slave of a black, barefoot and sullen, whom they called Dessalines. They scarcely knew one another. But each sensed in his comrade a kindred mood. The old coachman, who was known among the plantation slaves of his neighborhood as "the Physician," so great was the learning he had crammed into his ridiculously high and narrow head in his half-century of life, watched ap-

provingly the play of the heavy muscles in the
bare breast of Dessalines. And Dessalines, who
kept a respectful distance and never quite dared
lift his eyes to the face of the older man, knew
in his half-savage African heart that here in this
new and unhappy world the tricks, the indirec-
tions, and the careful wisdom that Toussaint had
put away were vital to their mutual cause. They
did not speak of that cause, but none who walked
in the straggling, silent line behind the bobbing
pipestaffs that bore the heads of Ogé and Chavannes doubted afterward that cause there was,
a cause to kill and burn and die for.

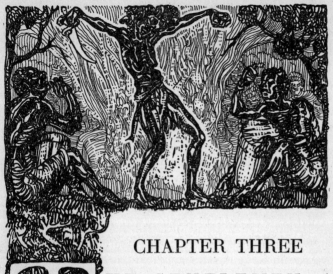

CHAPTER THREE

THE GENTLEMEN of the Provincial Assembly who had so anxiously watched the gray-brown faces of the freedmen the afternoon of the execution differed as to what they found there. Some discussed the question at the Crown Hotel that evening, gesticulated, and swore between loose lips wet with a fury of contempt. Their sallow faces grew hard and lined with a restless, unadmitted fear. Perhaps young Christophe's long-fingered hands gripped the tiny tray he carried with a tighter grasp than usual, but beyond that he showed no sign of hearing. The belief that negroes were things far short of human was by no means insincere. The blacks, who were present in some capacity at every private and public council, found this extremely useful.

The politicians of France resented the fashion in which their rulings had been set aside. Soon an order came giving to the free mulattoes the right of seats in the Provincial Assembly. It was a move scarcely aimed to strengthen the allegiance of the aristocrats who owned the sugar lands. Two regiments were sent from home to assist the new colonial governor to make a stand against the rebellion of the planters. But the soldiers deserted to the royalist camp and the governor was forced to leave the capital, Port au Prince, for the greater security of Cap François. The mulattoes in the south and in the west immediately organized and gathered by torchlight on the estates of rich *affranchis*. And in the hills behind Port au Prince, on remote plantations on the desert plains in the west, and in the distant communes of the north, scattered handfuls of slaves began to arm themselves with billhooks and cane knives, to fire and murder and chant the new cry of freedom. A very powder-barrel of a colony: the whites against France, the mulattoes against the whites, and the sullen, full-mouthed, hating blacks against the world. . . .

The black conspirators were most active in the north. Hardly an *atelier* in the extent of the great Plaine du Nord behind Cap François but had some self-appointed leader to whom the slaves looked for deliverance. All the plotting took place in secret, for the memory of the fate of Ogé and Chavannes had not died out. But while the whites, even though events had warned them to be preternaturally watchful, saw nothing, heard nothing, and scarcely found excuse for suspicion, an army and a complete organization came into existence in their back yards, in their kitchens, and in the sleepy, sweltering cane fields.

A code language, brought from Africa by the first slaves and nourished for two centuries, carried news to every black who had given evidence to the leaders that he might be trusted. Songs that had grown commonplace on the plantations carried new refrains which the careless ears of the whites could not detect. A phrase, an intonation in the melody, sung by a solitary herdsman or a black watchman at a sugar mill; a trick of the drum beat when the field workers gathered at the week's end for a dance under the watchful auspices of the estate foreman; a whisper; a tiny gesture—all served their purpose.

A negro leader named Boukmann, seeking something to bring his still fearful people to the sticking point, gave word that the King of France had proclaimed three holidays each week and put an end to whipping with the cat-o'-nine-tails—that their masters refused to obey. The blacks believed, but could not forget Ogé and Chavannes. They, too, had acted on the authority of that same King of France. In desperation the same leader added that a huge army was that same hour bound overseas from France to help them punish the disobedience of the planters. The excited talk in the compounds and the fields grew to a subdued bedlam at the delightful prospect—but still those who were to be responsible for giving the signal for open revolt kept silent, doubting what reliance could be placed in courage born of so illegitimate an ancestry of lies. On the night of August 14th Boukmann called a conclave of the leaders. They met, nearly two hundred of them, each one of whom had crept away under the cover of dark from a different plantation, in a dense bit of forest called Bois Caiman—the Alligator Wood —on a plantation in the Plaine du Nord.

Boukmann had set the stage. A half dozen torches stuck in the earth illumined with dancing flares of light a floor of pounded earth at the foot of a buttressed tree. Dark forms that emerged from the deeper darkness found places and crouched without a word, their eyes on the face of the leader. Without confusion, scarcely with outward evidence of the passion that made the fleshy lips in the crouching ring of men grow hard, they completed their arrangements down to the last meticulous detail, even the hour when the signal for the destruction of the whites should sound.

Then, when the talk was almost over, a thunderstorm massed up and obscured the remote starlight above the leaky roof of the jungle. Rain came down in a deluge, dousing all but a few carefully tended torches. Thunder muttered down the rain-drenched valleys. Sudden floods of lightning silvered the mountain peaks—and, as if born of the darkness and the storm, a giant negress appeared in the midst of the crowded open space. A long knife gleamed wet in her upraised right hand, her naked body was streaked with rain.

Slowly she began to sway in the movements of a dance regulated by some unheard rhythm

within herself. It was a rhythm recognizable to
all as one of the secret, unforgotten things of
Africa treasured through the years of slavery.
She sang a song, a song of the snake-gods, of
the great, immortal lovers of the black man, his
old-time friends who dwelt in storm and sky
and woods and now stood ready to help or hurt,
to be won by courage, to be appeased with blood.
As her voice rose to a screaming moan, a tusked
boar ran headlong, blinded and confused, into the
clearing. With a movement so sudden the
staring eyes around could scarcely discern it, the
priestess flashed her knife down. The boar, with
a squeal, slashed open from throat to groin, rolled
over dead. In a bowl lifted quickly to her the
woman caught the warm blood. With appropriate incantations she handed it round the inner
ring of men. Each drank and, as his lips touched
the blood, swore by the name of Papaloi, the
snake-god of Africa, that he would give his life,
if need be, to the cause of black rebellion. Boukmann was a high priest of voodoo, known and
feared throughout the Plaine du Nord. . . .
Toussaint, famous for his Roman Catholic piety,
drank with the rest.

Eight days later, at ten o'clock in the evening
of the 22d of August, 1793, a tomtom drum on

Turpin plantation, Boukmann's home, suddenly broke the peace of the starlit tropic night. It carried a new, wildly lifting melody. Across the valley another took it up, then another farther on, and in an instant two hundred hidden drums on as many plantations were beating out the tune. Two thousand square miles of the rich farmlands of Saint Domingue throbbed with a foreboding, spreading mood. In two hundred great houses set back among the mango trees, whites came suddenly awake. Before the night was over the stars were extinguished by the glare from a hundred fires. An exact historian states that during the week which followed six hundred coffee plantations and two hundred sugar refineries were given to the flames. An incalculable number of whites were dragged from hiding and slaughtered in the most frightful fashions the slaves could conceive—or recall from their own extensive experience in torture.

For eight days bands of slaves held a carnival of revenge—and were then defeated at the gate of Cap François. Boukmann was taken and his head impaled on a pole.

Toussaint, who succeeded Boukmann as leader of the blacks, sought an honorable peace for the rebellious negroes who still hid in the dense forests on the mountain slopes. He failed chiefly because there was now no stable government with which he could treat.

Three commissioners equipped with complete powers reached Saint Domingue. The King of France dropped his head into a basket. The colored men allied themselves definitely with the cause of the Republic of France, and Christophe, the inn servant, married the fifteen-year-old daughter of his employer, the negro Coidovic. Her name was Marie Louise.

In the same year, 1793, France went to war with Spain and England. Toussaint and the other leaders of Boukmann's rebellion crossed over into the Spanish half of the island and became generals in the Spanish army. They soon began to overrun the French territory they had so lately left as runaway slaves. And the whites, to complete the treason, appealed to England to invade Saint Domingue and protect them from the mulatto army that was warring with such conspicuous relish in behalf of the Republic. The civil commissioners, seeking a desperate cure-all, granted general freedom to all slaves in Saint Domingue.

From the maelstrom of events the least expected and the solitary thing of deep importance emerged—the freedom of the blacks. The whites and mulattoes had followed their courses in pursuit of opposite goals; the history of Europe had turned a somersault while the blacks had continued their inarticulate fight. But no one had particularly heeded them. Few thought much was seriously amiss that could not be remedied by eventual swift punishments. But an army faithful to Republican France was badly wanted and granting freedom to the slaves seemed the only sure way of recruiting it.

The beginning of the year 1794 found Saint Domingue in a sorry state. The Spanish armies under Toussaint and the other negro leaders held almost all the northern and eastern regions of the colony. The English, who had gladly come to the assistance of the rebel white colonists, held Port au Prince, most of the western seaboard, and important positions at the extremities of the northern and southern peninsulas. The commissioners who had granted universal freedom were home in Paris, explaining their extraordinary move to a government little interested in anything that transpired more than a league or two from the banks of the Seine.

A French Republican general was attempting to expel both invaders, realizing his efforts were doomed to failure. . . . Then Toussaint made up his mind that the aim of his long life's ambition, negro freedom, could best be achieved by alliance with the French, and turned a sudden right-about. He quit Spain for France, and began to fight back over the same territory he had so lately won. In a campaign scarcely equaled for its vigor in all military history he led his ragged legions of ex-slaves over the towering mountain ranges of the north, stormed a dozen towns, and raised the tricolor over each, proclaiming, as he advanced, the universal emancipation of the blacks.

Toussaint had no desire for the political independence of Saint Domingue. That dream had not yet been born. Toussaint spoke French as his mother tongue. All his education had come out of books written by Frenchmen. He hated the cruel aristocrats who had made slavery a horror on the island. He hated the planter who had buried nine black men up to their necks in the earth and then invited his friends to a game of bowls, with iron cannon shot for balls. But with devoted fidelity he loved the master who had been kind to him and he loved the men of Paris who had proclaimed the glorious creed of liberty, equality, fraternity. It was unnatural for him to fight for Spain, the enemy of his own country. It was natural for him to return to the tricolor cause when it had given proof in practice of its promises for human brotherhood. It was easy, too, for "the Physician," the beloved and admired of all the slaves who knew him, to transfer over-night the allegiance of his army.

General Toussaint, with the astonished eyes of the world upon him, came with his army within a few hours of Cap François, one of the few towns in the north he had not taken for Spain. He was received, by all but a handful of dis-gruntled royalists, as a deliverer. Regiments of black recruits flocked to his standard. They were glad to quit the work of the fields and sugar mills and were avid for a chance to fight the battles of the mother country that at last had declared against the vain, cruel gentlemen who for generations had compelled fourteen hours of work each blazing tropic day.

Among the first of the volunteers was Henry Christophe, the inn servant. He had watched, learned much, and waited long. Now at last the wheel of black men's fortunes had spun and paused to his liking. Toussaint, now dubbed L'Ouverture because of the almost uncanny gift of "opening" everything before the avalanche of the military operations, had known young Christophe and marked him as a likely man. Henry, who was twenty-seven, received the rank of sergeant and was put over a small band of men.

In the swift rush and shift of fortunes which filled the ensuing years Christophe disappears, to emerge seven years later as a general second only to the great Toussaint himself in rank, governor of the city and region of Cap François, and owner, so they say, of the richest, most superbly furnished mansion in the town. . . . In those seven years Henry Christophe had learned to write his surname. When he became king he learned to sign the "Henry," too.

CHAPTER FOUR

IN SEVEN years the slaves of the fields had created a kingdom. Toussaint, the coachman, was Governor-General and ruled over the whole island. No one before him had succeeded in uniting both the Spanish and French settlements and the all but impassable mountain ranges under a single rule. Never in the history of the world has as barren a human field yielded in a little time so marvelous a flowering of greatness.

The slaves had come from a thousand hidden towns and many hundred jungle tribes of Africa.

They had been brought in chains to a new and hateful world. Here they were barred from communication with their fellows until all picked up the awkward patois French that became the common tongue of the plantations. Through two long centuries they had been degraded by cruelty, weariness, and homesickness almost below the level of humanity. Yet, when the hour struck, they were ready and leaders were found most strangely touched with genius.

There was Toussaint, who conquered the armies of Spain, drove the English into the sea, and rose through every military honor till at last he had won for himself the unprecedented rank of Governor-General of Saint Domingue for life, with the privilege of choosing his successor; Jean-Jacques Dessalines, the African slave of a black, ferocious, unlettered, who achieved the rank of a general in the proud army of France and became governor of a province; Henry Christophe, black slave boy and stable hand who climbed with meteoric rapidity from the rank of sergeant to that of general and military governor of Cap François; Alexandre Sabes Pétion, the bastard son of a white French artist and a mulatto woman, scholar, soldier, painter, and lover of his people And there were twenty others of

·[40]·

almost equal prominence who rose from the ranks
of the mob-like army of the blacks.

For seven years of continuous, confusing,
costly war these men had led their ragged armies
against Spain, against England, and, unhappily,
often against one another—while in France a
pale, vain little Corsican ran like a fire over
Europe before the tornado of his own ambition.

In the first year of the nineteenth century
France under the First Consulate of Bonaparte
found herself at peace for the first time in a
decade. The armies that had conquered Europe
were idle. Insatiate Bonaparte was faced with
the realization that rich colonies must be found
for the wealth and energies of France if that
wealth and energy were to continue. Saint
Domingue, once the most important overseas
resource of Europe, had slipped somehow
through his fingers. The great sun-warmed
plains and hillsides that once had sent an unend-
ing procession of merchant ships laden with sugar
and coffee to all the ports of Europe were now
barren tracts of ashes and rank weeds, cultivated
sparsely by black men who sent their produce
to the United States and England And over
all these blacks reigned a little negro who had

won powers which within his lesser scope surpassed that of Napoleon himself.

There were many men in Paris who formerly had been planters of Saint Domingue. Now peace had come and profitable occupations were scarce, they thought pensively of the wealth and ease they so unwillingly had left behind. Men were found who were close to the First Consul. They poured into his ears continual tales of Toussaint—who had first made himself dictator and then sent an envoy to Napoleon to tell him of the change in the government of Saint Domingue, without a word of "by your leave."

Soon Napoleon gave orders that six of his greatest shipyards should set to work at once to prepare the greatest fleet France in all her history had ever dispatched across a sea. Eighty-six ships of war were to carry 22,000 soldiers—the pick of the army that had conquered Italy and Austria. Surely Christophe, Toussaint, and Dessalines, the three slaves who long ago had watched another fleet of France in the roadstead of the Cap, must have sensed the flattery, found substance for wonder and pride and a strong faith in their great destinies.

Napoleon, because he had black men to deal with, and therefore fools, he thought, sought out

two young sons of Toussaint's who were in Paris.
He found time to have them come to his palace,
where he talked with them and their tutor, a
white Frenchman named Coisnon. The two
young negroes had been at school in France for
six years and they knew little of what had happened in Saint Domingue. The flattery of an
audience with the greatest man in Europe and
his courtesy toward them made a profound im-
pression upon the two young negroes. He told
them deliberate, foolish lies to be repeated to
Toussaint, of his intention to continue the freedom of the blacks and his wish that Toussaint
understand the fleet came not to fight him, but
to "cause the name of France to be respected
among the enemies." Toussaint's sons embarked
with the expedition when it sailed not long after,
fired with a patriotic wish to show their father
the error of his ways.

The expedition seemed to most of them a sort
of happy aberration of the First Consul's to be
enjoyed while it lasted, but surely not to be taken
so seriously as the extent of the expedition indicated.

Charles Victor Emmanuel LeClerc, Captain-
General of the expedition, looked upon fortune
as singularly kind. In a time of meteors, his

whirl across the sky of Europe had been luminous
second only to Napoleon himself. First a volunteer, then a captain, and soon a general, he had
achieved great fame in Italy and won as prize
Pauline, Napoleon's own sister.

In that winter of 1802, when the expedition
sailed, LeClerc was thirty and Pauline, who went
with him, was only twenty-two. They had married five years before. LeClerc wore splendid
whiskers down his cheeks to add dignity to a
youth the older soldiers found somehow offensive.
Pauline, who was slender and beautiful and gay,
was quite content to look her years. The world
lay at their feet.

Bonaparte was surely destined to rule the
world, and, just as surely, he could be depended
upon to present some pleasant part of it to his
friend and general and brother-in-law. Saint
Domingue? No doubt a rather charming place.
The flagship of the fleet was laden with tapestries
and furniture and all the pleasant, rich acces-
sories that went to make a palace worthy of rela-
tives of the First Consul. As soon as these
blacks could be induced to get back to work
Napoleon would no doubt need a governor-
general, though he had not announced what future plans he had in mind. Saint Domingue

would serve well enough till an even more splendid corner of the world should want a ruler. If only those fellows hadn't painted such an exaggerated picture of Toussaint's strength! Two thousand picked men would have been so much less of a nuisance than twenty-two thousand.

On the morning of February 3, 1802, LeClerc and the larger part of the fleet arrived in the open sea off Cap François. Three other divisions, each under a different general, were at the same time preparing to attack at other strategic points on the coast.

LeClerc, as soon as the great promontory at the western end of the bay was sighted, gave an order for the ships to come to rest in the open sea. Then he sent a young ensign named Lebrun to tell Christophe to prepare the town for his reception.

The small boat in which Lebrun approached the shore was hailed from a fortress on the extremity of the point. He made a landing on the narrow shale-strewn beach and was greeted by General Christophe, whose reserved dignity, it is said, quite overwhelmed the young Frenchman. As they mounted the steep slope to the fort Lebrun noticed that a whole battery of cannon had been placed on the highland overlooking the narrow entrance to the bay. Every soldier of the garrison carried an unlighted torch.

Christophe, magnificently garbed in the full-dress regalia of a General of France, received Lebrun with somber courtesy. In silence they drove through the city to the governor's palace. As they rode along Lebrun, as if by accident, let fall a packet of printed handbills that were picked up and quickly circulated through the crowd. This did not, as Lebrun hoped, escape the notice of Christophe.

Lebrun bore letters addressed to Toussaint. He refused to put them in Christophe's hands. He had no message for him, he said, except Captain-General LeClerc's order to deliver the town at once. But he whispered to Christophe, "LeClerc will cover you with honors if you will deliver the town before Toussaint comes!" It had been agreed in Paris that the black officers could be cheaply won.

Christophe drew himself up to his great height. The afternoon sunlight streaming through the palace windows glinted against the golden epaulettes upon his shoulders. His full, reverberant voice came so that all in the great hall could hear.

"You think me capable of betraying my trust?

Citizen, I am a soldier. Governor Toussaint
is my chief. I will recognize no other authority
until he has told me himself that France has
properly replaced him. . . . You, Citizen, will
spend the night with us and to-morrow I will
return you to your General. I am dispatching
messengers to Governor Toussaint. Until I have
word from him you will keep your ships safe out
of range of my cannon."

The young aide-de-camp went off the next
morning to the flagship outside the harbor to tell
the astonished officers that he had dined that
night off plates of gold served by pages and that
the great banquet hall of the ex-stable boy's
palace was hung in draperies of brocaded silk.
He reported that the mayor of the city, a negro
named Télémaque, enthusiastically favored
LeClerc, that the 2,000 white residents of the city
were ready to receive him with avid hospitality.
Lebrun surprised them by saying that Cap François was such a city as no one dreamed to find so
far from home, a city with wide streets, rich
houses, a theater where the nightly play was well
attended, and great levees at the Governor's palace commonplace. Pauline was delighted. The
musicians, clowns, and players she had brought to
save her from dullness were charmed at the

thought of the *salons* that might be gathered, even here.

But LeClerc was impatient. He wrote:

I learn with indignation, Citizen-General, that you refuse to receive the squadron of the French army which I command, under the pretext that you have no order from the Governor-General. . . . I avow it will distress me to have to count you among the rebels. I warn you that if to-day you have not delivered all the batteries of the coast, to-morrow at daybreak 15,000 men will be disembarked. . . . I hold you responsible.

General of the Army of Saint Domingue
and Captain-General of the Colony
LeClerc.

Christophe replied:

I have dispatched one of my aides to Governor L'Ouverture to inform him of your arrival. Until his reply reaches me I cannot permit you to disembark. If you have the force with which you threaten me, I shall offer you all the resistance which characterizes a general. If the chance of war favors you will only enter the city of the Cap when it has been reduced to ashes, and even upon the ashes still will I fight you. . . . As to the troops which you say you will disembark, I look upon them as so many cards which the least wind will blow down. . . . As to the loss of your esteem, General, I assure you I do not want it at the price you put upon it, if it must cause me to act contrary to my duty.

I have the honor:
H. Christophe

Black Majesty

The letter was dictated. But the bold signature at the bottom was scrawled by the black slave who could not read what he had caused to be written.

There was another exchange of letters, with no increase in diplomatic phrasing on either side. Two days later LeClerc carried out his belated threat and landed his troops. But of the 800 splendid buildings that had composed the city, only 60 were standing. Christophe, too, had kept his word and burned the town. The tearful pleas of Mayor Télémaque, the petitions of the townspeople, the open threats of the 2,000 whites, and the desertion of a good number of the soldiers of his own regiment had not dissuaded him. Christophe never changed his mind. And, till the day he died, no one within sight of the fire of his hypnotic eyes or in sound of his imperial, booming voice ever dared to disobey him. He himself had lit the first torch. With his own hands he had put the flames to his own house, the richest on the island. With it he destroyed all the wealth he had accumulated during the period of Toussaint's ascendency, making himself homeless. But the flames that gutted his paneled walls and melted down his golden plate caught the town, blazed across a world, and gave challenge of war to Napoleon himself—Napoleon who had never known defeat.

When LeClerc landed, it is said that Pauline and her entertainers burst into unhappy tears at the sight of the ruined town. Henry watched them from a hidden eminence in the jungle-covered mountains behind the city. Then with a handful of soldiers he went through the hills to join Toussaint and plan a way to conquer destiny.

CHAPTER FIVE

WHEN Christophe declared war on Napoleon, burned the city of Cap François and retired into the hills, he could name few men who were faithful to him. His supplies were what they carried in their hands. But he was armored with a powerful thing. Christophe had discovered scorn.

LeBrun, the messenger General LeClerc had dispatched from his war squadron, had dropped handbills for the townsfolk to read. They proved to be copies of a proclamation by which Bonaparte hoped to make the blacks believe the war-

ships came only to insure their freedom.
Christophe knew it for a pinch of dust blown
in a sullen dragon's eyes.

"Whatever your origin and your color, you
are all free and equal before God and man. . . .
Welcome the French and rejoice to see your
friends and your brothers from Europe. . . .
Rally around your Captain-General; he brings
you peace." Then: "Whoever dares act inde-
pendently of the Captain-General will be a trai-
tor to his country and the anger of the Republic
will devour him as fire eats up dried sugar
cane!"

Napoleon had gestured crudely.

An eternal, drowsy quiet pervades the mountains and the rich green valleys of Haiti. It is
unsuited as a scene for war. The screams of
wounded men and the roar of bronze cannon melt
into echoes that dim away into silence as quickly
as does the tinkle of a cowbell or the song of a
negro laborer at work in the furrows of a slanting
field.

Christophe, Dessalines, and Toussaint found
it hard to realize that they were again at war.

After the burning of the Cap, Christophe had
retired to a sheltered valley thirty miles back
from the sea. Dessalines was encamped in the
arid plains behind Saint Marc, a port on the
western coast of the island. L'Ouverture was
moving with the swiftness of which he was a master across the mountainous mid-section of the
colony. Couriers who knew the shortest routes
through the maze of hills kept them in communication—but they carried tidings that Saint
Domingue was displaying no taste for resistance.

The "cultivators," slaves whom the events of
the past decade had turned into peasant farmers,
were out of sympathy with the generals. Under
Toussaint's rule the soldiers had been the privileged class. If the soldiers wanted to put their
heads into the lion's mouth of an infuriated
France, let them fight their own battles. The
whites, too, were cordial to the French. And
the mulattoes, the former freedmen, were more
friendly to LeClerc than any of the rest. They
had always been free. . . . Therefore the leaders
and their soldiers were alone.

Even the generals were defying France for
different reasons. Dessalines, born in the jungles

of Africa and transported as a slave, had a store of memories to draw on.

Toussaint fought for fear and pride. He loved France and her traditions, but he loved his weary, dull-eyed people far more. He feared with a kind of frenzy that slavery would begin again. And the old man had drunk of power. If only the young conqueror had seen fit to show him some slight homage, if only Napoleon had troubled to answer so much as a single one of the letters he had written telling of the conquests he had won for France—then he might have trusted him.

Henry Christophe fought for a triple cause. In a measure, he shared the hatred of Dessalines, more fully he agreed with Toussaint, but primarily he despised Napoleon. For a decade he had heard stories of the marvelous little artillery-man who had vanquished so many armies. Then the squadron came to rest outside the bay of Cap François and Napoleon stood revealed through messages signed with his own hand as a petty cheat devoid of justice and even the pride young Henry thought fitting in a fighting man.

No time was wasted. LeClerc, furiously angered by the burning of Cap François, resolved to hasten the routing of the blacks.

A large detachment dispatched to "arrest" Christophe was effectively checked, and won only the ashes of another town.

In the west, Dessalines, confronted with a superior force, fought valiantly though briefly, and retreated, burning everything in his line of march—towns, fields, estates and mills.

LeClerc hastened to follow the instructions of Bonaparte.

Abbé Coisnon, the tutor under whom Toussaint's sons had studied in Paris, went with them to a country farm where Madame Toussaint awaited her husband. L'Ouverture did not come at once, so Coisnon had an opportunity to pour into her ears his tale of Napoleon's devotion to the negro cause. When the old man arrived, Coisnon, his sons, and his wife urged him to surrender. They told him he was mistaken in looking upon France as an enemy.

Toussaint listened, torn by indecision. He sank into a chair in the parlor of his little house. Beneath the scheming eyes of Coisnon he ceased to be the conqueror and governor and sobbed like a tired old man agonized by loves that twisted him. He knew that if he kept faith to his people, his sons must go back to LeClerc, perhaps to pay forfeit with their lives. And perhaps the freedom of the blacks was not at stake. Then his sacrifice would be vain. How cruel if lives were lost to balm the hurt pride and the foolish fears of an old black slave.

He retired into an adjoining room to compose himself and reach a decision. After a little he came out, master of himself.

A number of his officers and several members of his family were awaiting him. He shook his head. He would prepare a letter to LeClerc explaining his stand.

He withdrew again and while the others slept he wrote all night. In the morning Coisnon returned to the Cap with Toussaint's sons.

LeClerc, chagrined, declared Toussaint and Christophe "outside the law."

The war went on. It had been thundering in a dozen places while Coisnon urged Toussaint to take credence in Napoleon's pacific aims.

The French, in the month that followed, never lost a victory, but they lost men, morale, and temper. The white troops were disturbed and uncertain. They were good Republicans whose lives for the past decade had been devoted to the cause of liberty. It troubled them that when they marched to meet the negroes in battle their antagonists sang *La Marseillaise*. Sometimes the opposing lines would sing in unison, audible and strange above the cannon and the cries of the dying.

Every day the negro generals lost nearly as many soldiers by desertion as through the natural casualties of war. The coolness of the peasant class changed gradually into active enmity. Many joined LeClerc's battalions.

But the hills were doing their part. The angry young Captain-General wrote to the Minister of Marine in Paris:

It is absolutely necessary to see the country to form an adequate idea of the difficulties which it presents at every step. I have never seen in the Alps any obstacles equal to those with which it abounds!

The blacks showed no symptoms of discouragement.

Dessalines summed up their mood: "Take courage, I tell you," he boomed at his ragged troops one roasting afternoon when the French had them besieged apparently beyond hope of escape in a little fortress in the foothills of the west. "The French cannot resist us long. Soon sickness will overtake them and they will die like flies. Hearken! If Dessalines surrenders a hundred times it will be to betray them a hundred times. I repeat, take courage! And you will see that when the numbers of the French have shrunk, they will not be able to guard the country . . . for we will always take refuge in our impregnable hills. They will be forced to quit it. Then I will give you independence."

Pauline was in Cap François. The people of the ravished town had built her a terraced palace on a promontory overlooking the wide bay. It had risen, a crude copy of perfection, almost overnight. There, surrounded by her entertainers, her Paris servants, and her ladies and gentlemen, she waited and wondered. She could not understand why their charming plans had gone so wrong. They had come, she thought, to govern a colony, to rest awhile beneath the tropic sun. And after two whole months her husband was still busy with a foolish war against some ugly blacks. What was the matter? Hadn't it all been arranged by her clever brother before ever they set sail? It was hard LeClerc found no time for her. . . . The days were fearfully dull. The frightened people picking despairingly among the débris of their ruined city were

·[58]·

hardly a cheering sight to watch from a mullioned palace window.

Then a letter came. Pauline's pale, pretty face lighted with the first smile it had worn in weeks.

LeClerc had routed the rebels. To be frank, they had all escaped—by the extraordinary expedient of walking under cover of night straight through the French lines. But no matter. LeClerc felt safe in throwing overboard the childish protestations by which he had sought to trick them. He declared the plantation lands restored to their rightful owners and added that slavery was to be returned at once to its old footing.

This was better news to send Bonaparte than tales of fruitless hill climbs.

The order proved premature. Tens of thousands of peasants joined General Christophe. With a vast avenging horde of half-naked people of the farms and hills, armed only with billhooks and hoes, Christophe swept across the north. News reached LeClerc that the negro camp fires were visible to the soldiers and civilians crowded amid the ruins of Cap François.

The Captain-General was stationed at Port au Prince when the news came. It is a long voyage from the Port to Cap François. It was quadruply long for the young general. He was pale, frightened, homesick for France and hungry for Pauline. As he walked the decks of his flagship he pulled at his burnsides till his long serious face turned from white to scarlet.

But Cap François was saved, for LeClerc and his fleet arrived in time.

He hastened to issue another proclamation. There had apparently, he announced, been a misunderstanding. The thing that lay nearest the heart of every Frenchman was freedom. He declared the freedom of the blacks in Saint Domingue would never be questioned, "Subject, of course, to the approval of my superiors in France."

Christophe, haggard from privation and the endless marching, was mending the army so sadly broken by his victories. When he heard the news his eyes narrowed.

A few days later he received a letter from a mulatto named Vilton, a man who had been his comrade in the army of L'Ouverture. Vilton was now a faithful officer of LeClerc's.

My dear friend [he wrote], with mortal regret have I watched your refusal to submit to the French general

whom the First Consul has sent to maintain the order which
you so successfully established in the city of the Cap and
in the region of the north. . . . You have sacrificed both
happiness and fortune. . . . Everyone, especially your
friends, believes you have had bad counsel and have been
ruled by the black chiefs who surround you. . . . M.
LeClerc is so persuaded that it was bad advice that caused
you to resist him that he is quite ready to pardon you if
you care to bring under his authority the troops which you
command and the position you hold. . . . We can guaran-
tee you a fortune and the peaceable enjoyment of it under
the protection of France in whatever country you choose.
. . . Quit your vagabond existence and abandon the cause
of an ambition which can come to nothing!

A sub-officer read the letter to Christophe. He
went apart from the clearing in the mountain
forest where his troops were bivouacked. The
great cockade hat on his head was shapeless from
many rains. The rich blue dye of his gold-braided
coat was faded from the fierceness of the sun.
His knee-boots were so torn his feet were almost
bare. He looked to where the men of his following crouched in whispering groups around the
cook fires. They now numbered less than three
hundred. Among them they could not have col-
lected perfect equipment for a single soldier.
They did not complain, but against the legions

of the French, swelled every day by fresh re-en-
forcements from Europe, they had nothing to
oppose but their passion, their contempt, and
their sweating, stalwart bodies.

Christophe strode to an eminence in mid-clear-
ing. He flung out his hands, stiff-fingered, tense.
All Saint Domingue had learned to watch those
hands. In the consciousness of his people they
had become the symbols of his strength. The
brown faces stared at him, dog-like. The hands
relaxed.

"Comrades," he said, "it is useless any longer
to fight the battles of our brothers on the field
of war. The cultivators everywhere are return-
ing to their farms. I will defend our cause hence-
forth in the councils of the colony. The French,
though they outnumber us a regiment to a man,
have learned to fear us. I will make a peace that
will do us honor. . . . But whatever comes, remember that these hills are ours, that they will
wait for us!"

That night Christophe dictated his answer to
Vilton:

I am ready to retract. But my doubts must be removed,
my suspicions cleared up. There is no sacrifice that I will
not make for the peace and happiness of my fellow-citizens

Black Majesty

if I am but convinced they will all be free and happy. Produce the proofs necessary for my conviction.

You speak to me of fortune. I no longer have any. Honor is the only possession now left me and my family. In friendship,

H. Christophe.

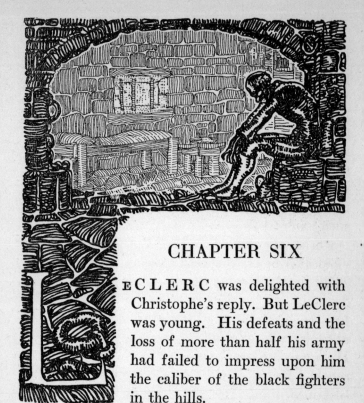

CHAPTER SIX

LeCLERC was delighted with Christophe's reply. But LeClerc was young. His defeats and the loss of more than half his army had failed to impress upon him the caliber of the black fighters in the hills.

He wrote Christophe:

Think of the essential service you could render the Republic by furnishing the means to secure the person of General Toussaint.

He showed General Christophe's answer to Pauline. They laughed together over it. The nigger stable-boy was proud indeed! The secretary who had penned the answer spelled queerly and Christophe's locutions were a trifle awkward. Such splendid words! "It would be perfidy and treason! A proposition so degrading to me is, in my opinion, a mark of your invincible repugnance to believe me susceptible of the smallest sentiment of delicacy and honor. Toussaint is my commander and my friend. Is friendship, Citizen-General, compatible with such baseness?"

Christophe proved coy, but LeClerc longed for victorious news to send to the impatient politicians in Paris. At Christophe's insistence he drew up and submitted to him a full law code for the governance of Saint Domingue which unequivocally guaranteed freedom to the blacks. He agreed to grant complete amnesty to all the rebels. He promised that Christophe would be sustained in his rank of General of Brigade and provided with an appropriate command in the French army.

The work of rebuilding Cap François had proceeded astonishingly. The town had recaptured some of its old gayety. Pauline's *salons* at her palace on the promontory were no longer marred by universal gloom.

When Christophe rode down from the mountains at the head of his tiny company the townsfolk were in a mood to do him honor.

Mulatto and negro women met him far outside the town gate. They were his neighbors and his friends. Some had known him as a waiter at the Crown Hotel. All had known him as governor of the city. His order, it was true, had set flame to their homes, but the tall young negro who rode so erect on his white horse at the head of the ragged regiment was their own. The long-fingered brown hands that lay relaxed on the white mane of the horse were negro hands that had gestured gorgeously before the face of Europe.

The streets of Cap François were bedecked with palm fronds, twigs of scarlet poinsettia and waving branches of bourgainvillea vine. Arches wound with flowers had been erected over street crossings. The little procession rode through a long channel lined at either side with French soldiers in parade uniform. At a signal every gun on every ship of the fleet in the harbor fired a salute. Captain-General LeClerc and his officers received Christophe in state on the broad terrace of Pauline's palace.

A few days later Toussaint, a broken, tired old man, rode into the city at the head of a few bedraggled regiments. His reception almost exceeded that awarded Henry Christophe. Dessalines followed. He, too, was received with honor.

But the high commanders of the French were angry and troubled to observe that when they received Dessalines, not once in a long interview did he look them in the eyes. He kept his head averted and his broad back turned rudely toward them. Dessalines long ago had sworn an oath that he would never look into a white man's face.

Christophe and Dessalines were installed in their new capacities as French generals. Toussaint L'Ouverture, his life-long ambition for the freedom of the blacks realized at last, voluntarily divested himself of all offices and honors, and retired to a small plantation in the arid plains near the city of Gonaïves, a port on the eastern rim of the bay.

Word went round the world that Napoleon's invincible armies had achieved another conquest.

LeClerc, before the surrender of Toussaint, had written him:

You, General, and your troops will be employed and treated like the rest of my army. With regard to yourself, you desire repose and you deserve it. After a man has sustained for several years the burden of the government of Saint Domingue, I apprehend he needs repose! I leave you at liberty to retire to your estates as you please. I rely so much on the attachment you bear to the colony of Saint Domingue as to believe you will employ the moments of leisure you may have in your retreat in communicating to me your sentiments respecting the means proper to be taken to cause commerce and agriculture to flourish once more.

One month later the frigate *Créole* was secretly dispatched from the Cap. Under cover of darkness she stood into Gonave Bay and let her anchor fall.

Toussaint had been invited to the home of a French general named Brunet to discuss with him certain points relating to the disposal of troops. He was received with courtesy and shown to a private room overlooking a balcony, to dress for dinner. In a moment a squad of soldiers with drawn swords entered through his window. The suddenness of their appearance dazed him. Then the realization swept over him that, lured by protestations of friendship, he had been led into a trap. In spite of their vaunted "words of honor" the French had come to take him. With a saber point against his heart the old warrior relinquished his sword—the sword that had not left his side in ten years of triumphs. He was carried with all haste and secrecy by back roads down to Gonaïves.

Toussaint was put aboard the *Créole* and it sailed to Cap François. In the harbor he was transferred in a small boat to the warship *Héro*. His wife and three sons, who also had been arrested, were put aboard with him. LeClerc hastily signed the *Héro's* sailing orders. She lifted her sails, caught the morning wind, and set her course for France. A few idlers, ignorant of her great cargo, for the news of Toussaint's arrest had been carefully kept secret, watched from the waterside of Cap François.

Toussaint, "The Opener," stood on the decks, his rakish cockade hat with embroidered gold braid on it held under a trembling arm. He saw the hills of his beloved island slip down over the world's rim forever.

Toussaint was ugly. He was small in stature, and slender with the frailty of sixty weary years. His narrow forehead was ridiculously high, his teeth were prominent. His bulging eyes stared

·[69]

from a brown face puckered in a lacework of fine wrinkles. Tears coursed down his cheeks. He turned to a French officer who stood beside him.

"In taking me away from my country, monsieur," he said, "you have cut down the trunk of the tree of black liberty in San Domingue. That tree will bloom again, for its roots are deep and strong." He bowed and went below to his cabin.

On the arrival of the *Héro* in Brest, Toussaint was permitted a hurried parting with his wife and three sons. Then he was taken and imprisoned in the Temple in Paris. After a little time he was transferred to the Fort de Joux, near Pontarlier, in the Jura Mountains.

He was never tried for any crime. He wrote many letters to Napoleon in which he besought at least the justice granted a common felon—if the savior of France's richest colony from her Spanish and English enemies did not, in their estimation, merit more. But Napoleon never answered, though several times he sent one of his aides to visit Toussaint in his dungeon to try to bully him into telling just where he had hidden a suppositious treasure of $40,000,000.

The aide found out nothing, for Toussaint would only shake his head dully and ask over and over again what had been done with his wife and his children. He never learned.

Toussaint had never in his life been beyond the eternal warmth of the tropics, but he survived one winter in a stone dungeon in the Alps. Then, in the spring, on the night of Wednesday the 27th of April, 1803, he died. No one had ever brought him news of what transpired in Saint Domingue. He went to sleep with a dream in his heart of crooning negro voices on the summer hillsides of an island far away. In the morning they found him curled up like a child on his pallet bed. The sweat of the walls had dripped down and puddled coldly on the floor. They had taken from him even the ragged remnants of the dress uniform of the Governor-General of Saint Domingue.

Napoleon had conquered.

LeClerc was young.

The old man had frightened him.

During the month which Toussaint had spent as a private citizen on his farm near Gonaïves, LeClerc's men had "intercepted" two letters the

"First of the Blacks" had written. Both might have been construed as innocent—but the young Captain-General thought not. They hinted, he fancied, at a renewal of rebellion. In one Toussaint said, "Providence may come at last to our assistance." . . . Providence was the name of the military hospital of Cap François. It was filling rapidly with dying Frenchmen. Yellow fever had begun.

LeClerc, immediately on the departure of Toussaint, gave an order for the disarming of the peasants. Six years before Sonthonax, the French Republican Commissioner, had distributed 20,000 rifles to the newly liberated slaves, saying: "Here is your liberty. Whoever tries to take these guns away will make you slaves again."

Christophe and Dessalines were intrusted with the delicate task. With their customary energy they disappeared into the mountains and hidden valleys of the north.

Saint Domingue was sweltering in the terrific, humid heat of an exceptional summer. The white European officers and men wanted nothing except to rest as quietly as might be near the seacoast, and were glad to leave the thankless business to the blacks. Christophe and Dessalines seemed faithful.

It amused the gentlemen of the high command to think how cheaply they had been bought—two bright new uniforms, two high commissions in the army of France, and those black rebels had been converted to devoted friends. It was just as he had told them, General Rochambeau remarked. He had been a planter in Saint Domingue before freedom had ever been heard of, so naturally he "understood niggers."

There was no doubt about it. In spite of the violent and often bloody protest of the peasants, Christophe was disarming them as fast as he could reach new districts. Several forts in the interior were overflowing with confiscated guns, he said in his reports. He had neither time nor men to spare for bringing them down to Cap François. "But I have them safe."

No echo of the young giant's laughter came down to the sea.

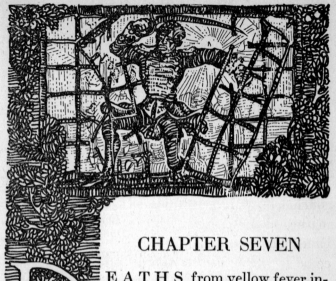

CHAPTER SEVEN

DEATHS from yellow fever increased. Soon the order for the disarming of the *indigenes* proved premature. It seemed to be the fate of all orders signed by the unhappy young Captain-General. An old kind of war broke out, with a new name for the enemy. Within a month news came from thirty places that as many bands of peasant "brigands" had flown to arms and were storming the French outposts, laying waste French farms, and murdering with insane fury every white man, woman, and child they could find.

Christophe and Dessalines found opportunity for a private conference. "Our hills will wait for us," one had said. And the other, "If I surrender a hundred times it will be to betray them a hundred times." They considered carefully.

The plague had scarcely started. Reinforcements by the thousand were still coming out from France. The brigand chiefs were fools, they concluded, and their raids as puerile and premature as LeClerc's orders. The conflict just ended had proved all too clearly that nothing could be accomplished without organization.

Christophe marched against the brigand leaders in the north. He knew the hills. Now he was equipped with the best guns, supplies, and munitions France could find. With the shock of a thunderbolt he fell upon them and saw to it the leaders were hanged.

Word came from Cap François that the young fool LeClerc was again unconsciously aiding the cause of rebellion.

He had instituted a reign of terror that would have shamed the Paris of Robespierre.

LeClerc had grown lank from worry. His high forehead was beaded half the time with unnatural sweat. The fingers that wound foolishly in his beard were as gaunt, white, and thin as those of a man whose years were double his own. He had begun to hate everything. He hated Rochambeau, stocky, violent Rochambeau, his second in command. He hated the general's big nose—like that of a cheap actor of tragedies. He hated his pomposity, his cocksureness, his cruel little pig's eyes. But, with so miserable a record of mistakes behind him, LeClerc began against his will to listen to Rochambeau's advice.

Rochambeau had lived in Saint Domingue. He knew the country, knew the "niggers." He said that no one of them was to be trusted. All were tainted by the mood of rebellion. They should be slaughtered like the worthless cattle they were. No half measures. Saint Domingue wanted a thorough house-cleaning. It was vermin-filled. It would be cheaper and more efficient to repopulate the island with fresh cargoes of docile blacks from the Guinea coast.

Rochambeau lifted his white fat hands. "Perish the blacks or perish the army. Make your choice, monsieur!"

Orders began to come from Pauline's palace. All brigand prisoners were to be executed. There need be no care wasted deciding who was rebellious and who was not.

Blood is vintage wine to men who are in mortal fear. Plague was riding swift over the sweltering, crowded town. The gods of Africa had sown a dread disease that rarely in history has affected a negro and has still more rarely spared a white.

Those who died of yellow fever during the day were wrapped in sheets and put outside the doors. At midnight creaking carts went through the empty streets, picked up the dead and hid them in great trenches in the fields beyond the city gates.

The officers of France turned dissolute. They found mulatto women, drank and whored with them. Life was as cheap as love. Sometimes the gaiety of the cotillions the officers held in the bare barrack halls was marred by a young lieutenant, stricken suddenly by the plague, slumping down through the brown arms that embraced him in the dance. Scarcely a single party reached its conclusion in the dawn before one or more of the guests lapsed grotesquely into death. But the dances always went on.

Out of revenge for nights like that, negro and mulatto prisoners by the hundred were taken aboard the ships in the harbor, manacled wrist to wrist in a long line and forced to jump overboard—to drag each other down to death in a tangled human chain of screaming desperation. When the supply of handcuffs ran short it was found convenient to cram the negroes into the ships' holds, batten down the hatches, and burn sulphur candles until they were suffocated. And when the military surgeon suggested that the bodies which the tide brought up on the beach were a source of dangerous contagion it was a still easier matter to force gangs of prisoners to dig deep common graves for themselves and then shoot them from behind so that they pitched into the pits.

Alexandre Sabes Pétion, a young quadroon, bastard son of a French painter and a mulatress of Port au Prince, held a commission in LeClerc's army. He had fought with conspicuous talent against Dessalines.

But it was becoming evident the whites would seek complete revenge against all blacks and "men of color."

One afternoon Pétion talked with Dessalines at the Cap. Both were soldiers, each admired the other's prowess and neither bore spite. Dessalines left the city to join his regiment and the quadroon rode out with him a little way along the road. They were an ill-assorted pair. Pétion, a thoughtful, educated gentleman, no darker than a white man burned by a few seasons of Caribbee sun. Dessalines, violent, heedless, unlettered and sooty black. But at the town gate of Cap François they shook hands. Then Dessalines lashed his horse and galloped into the mountains.

Pauline, frightened lest the fever stalk even to the palace of a Bonaparte, removed with her court to a small island a little way off the coast, safely beyond the marshy flats on which Cap

François was built. There she and her people found no trouble in forgetting.

Several of the youngest and most gallant officers who had just arrived with fresh troops attached themselves to her. Pauline began at last to enjoy Saint Domingue. LeClerc several times sent word that he was ill with fever, but he begged her not to be alarmed.

A French priest invited General Dessalines to dine with him. Some French officers, who wished for an opportunity to meet Dessalines, were coming. Dessalines was flattered.

He arrived at the priest's house to find the guests assembled and a long table set for a banquet with white linen, flowers, wine glasses, and tall candlesticks. The black General was to be the guest of honor.

As he stood talking, an old negro servant hobbled toward him carrying a bowl of water and a napkin He began to rinse his fingers. The officers courteously drew a few paces apart from him. Dessalines realized the old woman's eyes were beseeching his with blazing intensity. He

looked at her. Her lips and fingers moved in a
signal of the secret code learned by all the faithful blacks in the months before the leaders met
and drank the wild boar's blood at Bois Caiman.
Dessalines' beady eyes narrowed to fierce points.
He wiped his hands on the napkin and gently
thrust the servant aside.

He wrenched his sword from his scabbard.
With the sudden bellow of a wounded bull he
jumped to the banquet table and in five great
running strides reached its further end, leaving
a wake of smashed glasses and scattered silver.
His horse was tied just outside the window. In
a single leap he was in the saddle. Before the
Frenchmen could recover from their astonishment they could see him, the window frame
around his neck and his horse lashed to a frenzy,
disappearing down the sunlit road. His roaring
voice came back to them. *"Aux armes! Aux
armes! Vive l'indépendance!"* In an instant
they could catch responses already echoing down
the valleys.

A laborer in a field replied. A woman by the
door of a wattled mud hut on the hill above heard
and repeated the call. The Frenchmen paled and
looked at one another. Everywhere around them
faint but impassioned cries were troubling the

sunlit silence of the tropic afternoon. Within two hours 200,000 voices had joined in and the news had spread to every acre where men lived amid all the vast extent of the colony of Saint Domingue. The blacks, at last, were ready.

The old servant woman, still holding her napkin and bowl, slipped away unnoticed. She smiled proudly to herself. No one, perhaps, would ever know; but it was she who had saved Saint Domingue. The order had been given for the arrest of Jean Jacques Dessalines and she had warned him. Soldiers with swords in their limp hands were even then emerging crestfallen from their hiding place in an adjoining room.

For the first time there was unity. Pétion, accompanied by other mulatto officers, had deserted from the French, taking troops with him. Christophe held the 30,000 guns he had at LeClerc's order confiscated from the peasants and was ready to equip an army at the expense of disorganized brigands and frightened women. The cultivators, convinced at last that the reëstablishment of slavery was the aim of the French, were avid now.

The only response of the French to their new danger was to drown 2,000 negroes who were enlisted in all good faith in their army.

On the first of November—it was still the un-happy year 1802—just a fortnight after the re-newal of hostilities, young Captain-General Le-Clerc, completely confused and desperate, sank into the last unconsciousness of yellow fever. During the night he ventured alone into finality.

Pauline, supported by her weeping ladies, emp-tied her palace of all the fineries she had brought to costume a governor's lady and accompanied her young groom's body home to France.

Napoleon, out of family pride, had the coffin put in the Panthéon, the hall of heroes. Pauline for a time was inconsolable, but in the following year she married a prince of Italy and learned to laugh again.

Rochambeau succeeded to the command va-cated by LeClerc. He sent a ship to Cuba to bring back a cargo of bloodhounds. The train-ing of these beasts became his favorite amuse-ment. In public shows held on Sunday after-noons they were taught to tear the vitals out of black men and be docile to all whites.

In Europe, the vanity of Bonaparte had swollen too quickly. England, jealous and frightened of her neighbor, dispatched a fleet to the West Indies. Her warships barricaded the ports of Saint Domingue.

Rochambeau relinquished his hold on all positions in the interior and concentrated his resources in the coastal cities.

The negro and mulatto leaders agreed to an organized command under Jean Jacques Dessalines.

In the spring of 1803, Jean Jacques, with only victories behind him, leapt to an eminence before his troops, took a tattered French tricolor banner in his heavy hands, and rent it twice from top to bottom. In his left hand he held the blue strip, in his right the red. For years in the minds of the negroes of Saint Domingue the tricolor flag had symbolized the union of the blacks, the whites, and the mulattoes—blue, white, and red. Dessalines let the white strip float to the dust. He stamped it down and proclaimed, while the soldiers shouted hoarsely, that never after should whites share in the island's destiny.

At the end of a year's fighting the French held only Cap François and a fortified position at the end of the northern peninsula. Dessalines, Christophe, Pétion, and a dozen other rebel leaders were moving down upon them from the mountains above the Cap.

Five strong forts, garrisoned by fevered, despairing veterans, guarded all approaches to the town. An English war squadron was patrolling the exit from the harbor.

The armies met at dawn. Five black regiments made simultaneous attacks on as many forts, dividing the attention of the French. But the whites behind their battlements on the hilltops had heavy artillery to train on the ragged negroes who strove to scramble up the bare inclines toward them.

They mowed the attackers down like grain. A black captain named Capois had his hat knocked off by a rifle bullet. The next instant a fifty-six-pound cannon ball killed his horse under him. He struggled free from his stirrups, rose, and swinging his saber, shouted to his men to advance.

Rochambeau and his guard of honor witnessed the by-play. They broke into sudden cheers. A drum was sounded in the fortress and an hussar appeared, holding a white flag. The firing ceased. The messenger rode down to where the wondering Capois stood, his saber point resting on the ground. The Frenchman dismounted, clicked his heels, and bowed. "Captain-General Rochambeau," he said, "sends his admiration to the officer who has just covered himself with so much glory."

Capois bowed awkwardly. The messenger remounted and soon disappeared behind the wall of the fort. The invisible drum rolled again and the fight went on.

In the evening the French salients fell. Ten days later General Rochambeau and his officers were prisoners aboard the English ships and the negro armies entered Cap François.

The French had been driven into the sea, exiled forever from dominion on the western rim of the Atlantic. The slaves were masters.

Rochambeau, just at the end, had found his imported bloodhounds useful. They had been of little effect against armed soldiers, but when famine attacked the beleaguered town they served well as food.

Dessalines demobilized his army.

CHAPTER EIGHT

ON JANUARY 1, 1804, the army of Dessalines regathered on the desert plains near Gonaïves. The independence of Haiti (newly named by Dessalines after an old Indian name that meant "the high place") was to be officially declared.

Two learned mulattoes quarreled over the phrasing of the document. One of them composed an Act remarkable for its judicious weightiness. "What you have done," said the other, "does not fit our mood. To draw up an Act of Independence, we should have the skin of a white man for parchment, his skull for an inkwell, his blood for ink, and a saber for a pen!" and he wrote while the generals sprawled sleeping under the moon in the crowded town.

All night the roads and trails leading into Gonaïves were pounded by the bare feet of blacks come to hear the phrasing of the dream their Dessalines had fulfilled for them. Some wore only ragged loin cloths, others broadcloth coats or breeches, rarely both, taken from French soldiers killed in battle. The slurring sing-song of the mob's whispering, in the faulty creole French that was the common tongue of all the blacks, made the warm night vibrant. This independence the generals talked of—did it mean no more wars, no more work, free rum and flour? Jean Jacques would tell them.

At dawn when the generals awoke they found the mulatto huddled asleep over the table. Under his elbows lay an Act of Independence. But in spite of his scorn of the other man's effort, his Act was brief and rather pallid.

However, the great day had dawned. There was no time for further debate.

The Act was read in the presence of the generals in full view of the gathered army. To the sound of war drums and battered French trum-

pets, Dessalines, stiff-fingered, affixed his mark.
Christophe followed him and wrote down the only
word he had learned to write. The other generals signed their names in full.

Dessalines flung out his thick, short arms,
peered into the upturned faces of his adoring
people, and spoke to them of their victories, of
the hatred for France which must never dim, of
the land, the hills, and the future magnificence
that was theirs.

In the afternoon, a baking afternoon of fearful heat and fine white dust that made one's sweat
sticky, the generals did what was to be done.
They declared Jean Jacques Dessalines Governor-General for life, with the privilege of choosing his successor.

That night when the sun went down it was red,
close, glorious. Jean Jacques, child of the jungles, slave of a black, warrior, hero, conqueror,
had had his day.

Poor Jean Jacques. His secretaries began to
bring him papers. All day long they gave him
not a moment's peace. "What, Jean Jacques,

shall we do about foreign trade? About export duties? Land deeds? Jurisprudence? With what shall we pay the army? When?"

What did Jean Jacques know of these things? Sometimes in his impatience he would drive them out of his presence with a stick—then the problems of government would grow miraculously more easy for a space. But the conqueror was restless.

The high-ceilinged office of the State House, where his secretaries expected him to sit all day and watch the curtains flutter in the rare gusts of humid wind, was no place for Governor-General Dessalines. He cracked his knuckles, stared at the polished boots high on the desk before him, and brooded. Then he gave orders that all Frenchmen who still lived in Haiti were to be killed.

He rode himself, with the sweet taste of the tropical noondays in his mouth, to see his orders carried out. And carried out they were.

Christophe, who came second to Jean Jacques in authority, had been reinstalled in his old post as governor of the region of the north. He remonstrated at the massacres, but remonstrance was useless. Very well, then. Since Jean Jacques had so immutable a loathing for the

French, Christophe invited English traders to come to the Cap. He guaranteed them safety for life and property. Haiti must survive. Christophe knew the eyes of the world were on her, cynical, curious eyes, puckered at the corners with contempt.

In August, 1804, Napoleon took the title of Emperor. Two months later Dessalines followed his lead, and was crowned Jean Jacques le Premier—First Emperor of Haiti. A jeweled crown was set on his head—and the eyes that had seen so much during the swift journey from a thatched mud hut in the Guinea swamps to an emperor's palace on a great island on the southern seas, filled, they say, with puzzled tears of pride.

The secretaries and the gentlemen of the Emperor's Cabinet had at last learned not to trouble him. Jean Jacques now had palaces, and some were so ungrateful as to say that he furnished them too liberally with ladies. No one found fault with an emperor's having twenty mistresses, black, brown, and tan, but it was hard for a struggling state to be expected to spend twenty fortunes on them every year.

Jean Jacques's star was setting. Slowly, behind shielding hands, a snicker ran through Haiti. They were laughing at great Dessalines. The Tiger had taken up dancing.

He imported from France — from hated France— two mincing professors of the minuet. Hour after hour every day they tried to lead the sweating master of the blacks through the intricacies of the latest Paris dances.

Jean Jacques was squat and as strong as a gorilla, but he was not graceful. He could ride a horse at full gallop down a rock-strewn hillside under a raking cannon fire; he could swing a sword and rout an army with a bellow rent hoarsely from the cavern of his chest—but guide his feet in a minuet, not at all.

No one dared tell him he was clumsy. It would have been more dangerous than calling him a coward. But at state levees, at private entertainments, even at Cabinet meetings, he always made opportunities for displaying the grace he fancied he possessed. The generals, the mulatto politicians, and the mistresses in favor at the moment would applaud, while he swelled like a turkey cock.

He was far too busy to realize his state was falling to ruin through corruption, oppression, and disorder.

The long southern peninsula of Haiti, a narrow procession of steep, unfertile mountains, divided by a hundred precipices from natural intercourse with the rest of the country, had always been a center of rebellion. The old *affranchi* class was strongest there. In that region the prosperous mulatto planters had never accepted the blacks as their political or social equals. They scorned ignorant, fiery Dessalines and hated him for one of the few laws he had dictated—that all subjects of his Empire should be known as "blacks."

This outlawed more than a hundred words that had come into use to describe various shades of color and mixtures of blood. It had all been worked out with elaborate care. A man who could prove his veins bore 228 parts white blood to 94 parts negro felt himself the social superior of another who was known to be afflicted with 84

parts negro blood to only 112 parts white. And
Jean Jacques, the clown of the minuet, had
laughed at their little dignities! It was a thing
not to be forgiven even an emperor and a conqueror. The very governors and generals he had
appointed, who had risen to power under his protection and owed their authority to the luster of
his name, began to rise against him. The mulattoes in all parts of the Empire joined with them.
Murmurs of restlessness and gusts of laughter
grew to active civil war.

The southern peninsula fell to the rebels.
Word came to Emperor Jean Jacques, but he
angrily dismissed the messengers. More of their
tedious papers.

They were marching on Port au Prince. The
capital was doomed to fall at any hour, they told
him. Emperor Jean Jacques could not understand. They brought him news of a rebellion, but
no mention of battles, of charges, repulses, and
death. Was no one resisting, or had all the world
gone mad? Suddenly Jean Jacques began to
roar with the raging fury that had defeated
France. The sneaking yellow men had betrayed
him. He'd make all right and orderly with a
few swift saber strokes. He had but to ride

proudly in his finest uniform before his people and they would remember who was master.

He mounted his horse, gathered his personal staff about him, and started for Port au Prince.

The odor of a horse's sweating flanks was good to smell again. Jean Jacques had not lost the gift of wonder. These hills that made a ragged scroll against the sky were his. The valleys where the streams ran under bowing cacao trees were his—his! The slave of a negro grown to emperor!

The little cavalcade rode in silence under the dry heat of the sun. Only wind-twisted shrub and grotesque cactus bordered the road. Dessalines, because his horse was best and because he was Emperor of Haiti, rode ahead.

Before long the Red Bridge, a way point on the highway into the capital, appeared in the distance, blurred a little by the murky stratum of the heat mirage that lifted from the road.

Dessalines turned his head and shouted an angry question to the officers who rode behind

him. "Why has not the army ridden out to meet
me?" He brought his spurred heel irritably into
the flanks of his mount and faced forward.

The white road, empty an instant before, was
filled with soldiers who had sprung from hiding
in the ditches and from behind the dwarf trees
that bordered the way. They carried guns tipped
with flashing bayonets. The Emperor had ridden
into ambush. In an instant they were milling
about him, shouting, cursing. Dessalines knew
them, but he saw in their black faces a look that
he had never seen before—fury and hatred,
mingled queerly with terror. A mulatto officer
on the outskirts of the mob shouted an order:
"Shoot! shoot!" Fifty guns were lifted and lev-
eled toward the Emperor's head. But no one
obeyed.

A stout club hung by his saddle. He seized it
and shouted to the officers of his party to come
to his assistance. A single horseman charged
through the mêlée to a position beside him. From
the corner of his eye the Emperor saw the rest,
already small in the distance, followed by a rolling ghost of dust. With a great cry he swung
his club, knocking down the flashing bayonets
that thrust up into his face.

Only a long minute had elapsed. The soldiers under the flashing feet of the two frightened horses were silent and confused. They were in the presence of the Emperor. This man they had come to kill was great Dessalines!

The mulatto officers were dancing in rage. Their *coup* was failing. Dessalines and his one faithful officer were slowly forcing their way through the mob. Jean Jacques's ugly face was twisting into a proud sneer.

"Kill him! Kill him!" they yelled. And no one did.

Dessalines's club rattled the bayonets down, now and then landed dully on a skull. The Emperor laughed, an ugly, revengeful laugh.

A fourteen-year-old mulatto boy, who was hiding in some bushes at the roadside, lifted a rifle and fired. The bullet killed the Emperor's horse. Dessalines crashed down into the mob. His cheek by chance was laid open by a bayonet blade. In another second he was dead. An Emperor's blood splashed on common soldiers' dusty feet had given them sudden courage.

In their mad anger they tore off his fine uniform, lopped off the fingers, the arms and legs, and thrust a hundred wounds into the still flesh.

·[97]·

The one faithful officer who had jumped down to stand over his fallen master was slain.

Then, afraid, trembling with the horror of their act, the mob slunk off, leaving an officer and a squad of men to escort the Emperor the little remaining way into his capital.

Along the road as the procession walked toward Port au Prince, black peasants came out of their thatched mud huts, and asked the soldiers what was the ugly thing they carried in a bloody burlap bag. When they were told they fell silent. Soon old men found their drums, beat upon them, and through the silent, droning summer afternoon sent word across the mountains and over the fertile plains that Dessalines, the Tiger, was dead.

It was late when they reached the capital and they had wearied of their burden. They flung the body of Jean Jacques on the grass in the open square before the State House.

Children came and stared and ran away, wailing for the shelter of their mothers' skirts. A few black soldiers swaggered up and spat on what remained of the man who had given them freedom. But soon, as the sun went down behind a distant island in the bay, the idlers dis-

Défilée came into the place where the body of the Emperor lay. With a sudden sob the fluttering hands dropped still, her twisted, laughing face grew pitiful.

appeared and the broken body of Jean Jacques was left alone.

Then Défilée came. Défilée, "the Defiled One," was mad and a woman of the town. She was a butt for children's laughter and the snarls of dogs. Everyone knew her.

Défilée had grown old perhaps more quickly than her sisters, but the older and the madder the "poor fool" had grown the more she laughed. And the more she laughed the more she danced. The peasants who lived along the country roads where she wandered said her bare black feet, crusted with the white dust, were almost never still, and that with foolish flutter her hands kept time. She had no home. Her food she found on the trees that overhung the walls.

Défilée came into the place where the body of the Emperor lay and a gaping child told her what it was. With a sudden sob the fluttering hands dropped still, her twisted, laughing face grew pitiful. She threw her gaunt, half-naked body on the ugly thing that had been Dessalines. And after a little she put it back in its sack and, no longer dancing, carried it into the dark shadows under the trees of the cemetery.

The next morning they found her still guarding it, and drove her away. A friend of Dessalines dug a grave for him and marked it with a stone. Défilée disappeared. Wondering people, when they heard what she had done, remembered that long ago Jean Jacques had loved her, that through him she had won her name, Défilée, and by him had been taught to dance.

CHAPTER NINE

THE NEWS of the fall of Emperor Jean Jacques was brought by military messengers to where Henry Christophe governed the city and region of the Cap. His enemies say he smiled and made a quick French gesture with his mobile hands, as if to ring a curtain up on a part of the show in which he was at last to play the lead. His friends—and in that time they were in the majority—say he drove the dispatch bearers from him in a burst of fury, retired alone to a little chamber for a while, and when he joined his officers again, looked unseeing from a mask grown gray and old. Jean Jacques and he had been slaves together, both of them slaves of black men. Together they had seen the execution of Ogé and Chavannes, together grown to the stature of generals and masters of men. Christophe and the Tiger had been linked by too strange a destiny to sever with a gesture.

Whatever his first reaction to the news, on the same day Henry called his secretary and dictated a letter. It was addressed to the mulatto officer who had been chief conspirator against Jean Jacques.

The tragic events which you write me of give me great pain. . . . I have never, as you know, been dominated by pride or ambition. The happiness of my citizens [*the possessive came easily*] has always been my one desire. It would only be with great misgiving that I would accept the great burden which the unanimous will of my brothers has placed on me in confiding to me the reins of government, were it not for the firm conviction that your light and counsel will always come to my aid in case of necessity.

I therefore accept the task which is as honorable as it is painful and difficult. Tell my sentiments to the army. . . .

Henry had had opportunity to consider the faults of the Empire. He gave orders that a national representative assembly should be convened, and that it should draw up a republican

constitution and appoint whomever it saw fit as
ruler. He knew that 33 parishes in the north
could be relied on to elect representatives unequivocally behind him. These would safely bal-
ance the 23 parishes in the south and west
controlled by mulattoes none too fond, for social
reasons, of full-blooded blacks.

But when the Assembly at last met, after an
inexplicable and wasteful delay, the representatives from the north were astonished to find that
the mulattoes of the south, headed by Pétion, had
elected 41 representatives, a safe majority.

In an atmosphere of mutual distrust, they
quarreled and debated, and at last, on December
27, 1806, after a nine-days' wrangle, produced a
republican constitution and unanimously declared Henry Christophe President of Haiti—
but for four years only. A senate would appoint
the Cabinet. It, too, would make all laws and
control the army.

During the months of waiting, Henry Christophe had ridden over half the tortuous trails
and nearly all the roads of the north. A page
boy had always accompanied him, carrying a
brass telescope, once the property of a now dead
captain of Napoleon's fleet.

When they came to eminences they stopped

and through the lenses Christophe swept his eyes over the great plains, the hillsides, and the nestling whitewashed towns in the gorges. Wherever he looked there was the same drab spectacle. The fields were forests of bramble and weed, except where they were black from fire. Half the slopes had been raked and pitted by cannon balls and the towns were a confusion of broken mud walls and thatch that had wanted renewing for a decade. During the war times no one had farmed except to gather the cotton, coffee, sugar, plantains, and bananas that grew wild. Under the tyranny of Dessalines the cultivators, discouraged by the unhindered raids of the irregularly paid soldiery, had not thought it worth while to plant. Geometrically trenched fields, the smashing grind of macerators turning cane into sugar, these reminded them of the old days when white men and the hunger of the fertile land were masters. Now, were they not "free"? And what better thing was there to do with freedom than to sleep the drowsy days away, then dance through the night under the stare of the white moon?

The long-fingered negro hands that grasped the brass telescope grew white-knuckled with the intensity of his impatience. Soon, soon, he'd wipe

the scorn off the face of France! Not a man
but would be rich and happy. Not a meter of
land but would be turned in furrows, not a grain
loft empty or a mill not turning. The world
must be taught by example that the despised
"nigger" could take his place in the world.

Then the constitution came and proved to be
a futile work of jealous yellow men who lacked
the courage to recognize their need for a master.
Christophe summoned his troops.

Swift orders were given. In his richest uniform of peacock blue, edged with scarlet and embroidered with gold, with a huge half-moon hat
trimmed with a white ostrich feather on his head,
he rode before them, down toward Port au
Prince. Soldiers joined him all along the way.

He reached the city simultaneously with the
arrival there of the mulatto army of the south.

Christophe attacked and was repulsed.

Two days later he issued an order for his army
to right about and return to the north. The soldiers were to disarm and go to their homes.

Port au Prince, overcome by astonishment
and delight, was left to its own resources. They
had realized the city, except for a miracle, was
doomed, in spite of their first successful resis-

tance. But the miracle had occurred, a miracle born of a black man's vast impatience.

The army, with the same driving haste with which it had come, marched home and was disbanded. The men of the south, somewhat foolishly, picked up the shattered pieces of their pride and founded a republic.

Henry Christophe returned to his palace at Cap Haïtien (the name of Cap François too had been changed). At his order the civil and military leaders came together to draw up a constitution. There was little wrangling, for they knew what he wanted.

On February 17, 1807, the new constitution became law.

Christophe was chief governor. They made him generalissimo of the land and sea forces of Haiti and they bestowed on him the privilege of choosing his own successor, stipulating the choice must be made from among the generals.

"The choice must be secret," the constitution said, "and contained in a packet hidden away which is to be opened by the Council of State solemnly assembled for that purpose. The President must take every necessary care to indicate to the Council of State where the packet is put away."

He was to select his own ministers and suggest laws to the Council, and he could, without appeal, veto any they made. But it was clear the Council would be most unlikely to experiment. Almost the only duty of that body was to furnish a strict and detailed annual accounting of the money they had spent.

Catholicism was declared the official religion of the state—but with complete toleration of all other sects. Divorce was forbidden. Fathers and mothers, under the new law, had no right to disinherit their children. Haiti would not interfere with the politics of any neighboring colony. Foreign business men were assured absolute protection. And the salary of Henry Christophe was put at what was the equivalent of $40,000 a year, to be paid out of a treasury which did not exist.

Christophe was forty. Because his life had been so crowded and because despair had so often dogged him he already looked upon himself as old and he was tortured by the sense of the little time he had. He had never read a book and he could write only half his name. The only association he had ever had with educated men was when he was a waiter at the Crown Hotel and was privileged to overhear the talk of drunken

slave-owners and homesick soldiers of France.
But he had known Toussaint L'Ouverture and he
had watched Dessalines pitch down to disaster.

Haiti was bankrupt. Christophe sent letters
to the United States and to the European powers
offering opportunities for profitable trade. Haiti
had no currency system, so he created one.

After the destruction of the plantations and
the abolition of slavery, the black cultivators of
Haiti had grown more and more dependent on
wild produce. Their huts were made of mud and
sticks and palm leaves. Food grew wild or with
little urging. For utensils, bowls, spoons, and
bottles, the blacks made use of the fruit of the
gourd vine, dried in the sun, scraped clean of
seeds, and then cut into the requisite shapes. If
there was such a thing as an irreplaceable necessity in the careless life of the peasants, it was the
gourd, Christophe mused. Gourds were useful,
but they soon wore out.

Chief Christophe issued an arbitrary act which
declared every green gourd in northern Haiti
the property of the state. A new crop was just
ripening and soldiers were sent to every commune
to collect it. The peasants made no objection.
Christophe was their master now and whatever
he did was right.

Gourd vines grew over many garden walls. Others had flung a rank, concealing tangle over the ruins of houses burned by Boukmann's rebels sixteen years before. Another sort grew on prim, round-headed little trees. Without regard for quality or ownership, Christophe's messengers took them all and a great procession of laden burros and high-piled farm carts brought them into Cap Haïtien. Before long 227,000 green gourds and calabashes were deposited in "The Treasury." Christophe put a value of twenty sous on each.

The coffee crop was almost ripe. When the cultivators brought the dried berries into the capital, Christophe bought them at the current market rate and paid out his gourds, which by this time the peasants needed badly. Then he resold the coffee to European merchants for gold. Before the year was out the state of Haiti had a metal currency of absolute stability in circulation. To this day the standard coin of Haiti is called the *gourde*.

Christophe got word of a secret correspondence being carried on between some Haitians and certain mulatto malcontents in Jamaica, England's island colony to the southwest. A feeble plan designed to foment a rebellion there against the

British had been set on foot. Christophe sent soldiers to arrest the Haitian agitators, tried them himself, and sentenced them to the prison work gang. Then he took good care that the English should hear of what he had done.

England promptly entered into a commercial treaty with him and English merchants soon arrived to open trading stores in the Cap.

The outlook was favorable, but Pétion and his friends in Port au Prince had recovered from the shock of Christophe's triumphant march against them and had resolved to expand their territory.

The army of the Republic numbered nearly 10,000. As soon as Henry was safe at the Cap and his troops had partially disbanded, it sallied forth in leisurely fashion and occupied a number of towns at the rim of Christophe's dominion. Christophe marched against them and was victorious in a series of violent fights.

But the civil war continued for nearly five years. Christophe from the first had discarded any notion of extending his sway into districts not unanimously servile to him. But he was willing to accept a challenge. A violent personal animosity existed between the two leaders. Pétion, whose subjects were free from all restrictions, called Christophe a tyrant. In his speeches he was always careful to point the parallel between Dessalines and his successor. Both were absolute, black, and ignorant, and, he predicted, both would end in the same fashion. Christophe, for his part, took satisfaction in pointing out that the mulatto president had issued 4,000,000 worthless dollars, stamped out of tin, and that with the remark "all men are thieves" he had ceased all effort to stop the corruption of his ministers of state.

But at last the wasteful conflict drew to an exhausted close. No peace was made. But hints were coming from the other side of the Atlantic that France was finding too much comfort in their quarrels. If Haiti was to build impregnably, it behooved her to quit tearing down and set at once to work.

CHAPTER TEN

CAP HAÏTIEN was a shabby city. Only a man with an excellent memory could have said which way the streets, now filled with broken bricks and mortar, were supposed to run. Some little parts of each of the 800 buildings Christophe had burned were still standing; a gaunt wall, a blind window latticed with rusted iron, or a lonely garden gate that gave on heaps of stone, charred by fire and covered gratefully over with vines run wild. Goats, cows, pigs, and scrawny hens hysterically mothering broods of chicks, followed the zigzag paths through the ruins.

·[112]·

Black Majesty

Pauline's palace on the hill was empty. Old horses with slat sides, grown too old for usefulness, browsed on the weeds that grew through the chinks in the paved terraces and from the beds of the dry fountains. When a stone knocked loose from the slope above by the bare feet of a peasant woman rattled suddenly down on the sagging roofs, the horses would whinny, arch their necks, and gallop through the banquet halls. Black sows slept amid the mud and whitened weeds in the shadowy, molding chamber where Pauline and her young groom had slept.

The country presented the same spectacle of sorry disuse. Filthy negro shacks, three walls of which were mud and the fourth the side of a French planter's ruined mansion, were lost in a scrub jungle of coffee trees, sugar cane, plantains, and bananas grown ragged and unfruitful from neglect. Over all the region, far flung and once magnificent, hung the rank odor of defeat—a carrion world that stank of wood burned by fire, sodden by rain, then dried by the dead, heavy warmth of the tropic sun.

There was much to do.

·[113]·

From the sad procession of the years, a parade of men gone gladly down to death, two men who loved Christophe had stepped out. Now, with history behind them and only the gaudy phantoms of ambition in front, they had attached themselves to their leader. Wherever he went, they went too. Technically, they were his secretaries. In their hearts they were his impassioned lovers.

Pompée Valentin Vastey, the English traders said, could "almost pass for a white man." He was the bastard son of a white father whose memory he scorned and a mulatto mother he had forgotten. He was slender, small, and wore his reddish brown hair clipped short. His skin was the color of old parchment. But no one of his time had more tightly wound the fibers of his mind round the outcast dream of the negro's greatness. Vastey, the "white nigger," loved the blacks with a fierce, consuming love. And he hated all whites with a double fury.

Dupuy was gentler, except in the strength of his devotion to Christophe. Dupuy in 1811 was in his early thirties. He had served as a subaltern in Dessalines's army, had emigrated to the United States after the Tiger's accession to power, and had made a small fortune in business

in Philadelphia. But when he had heard that
Dessalines was dead and that Christophe was in
power, he had sold his Philadelphia "interests"
and come home to see what fortune held for him.

They always accompanied Christophe when
he rode over the mountain trails to visit the outposts of the state.

Once they stopped their horses, winded from a
long slow climb, on a ledge of a mountain. While
the horses nibbled the grass that grew beside the
path they stood together and looked at the world
spread at their feet. The sun, a brazen gong,
hung in the blue sky. The villages in the green
valleys were like toy towns. Through the utter
quiet of noonday faint echoes lifted up to them.
Somewhere, miles away, a negro cultivator was
singing a throbbing, high-pitched song of Africa.
A goat bleated. Blue-gray clouds of humid mist
were hanging motionless on the gaunt, distant
hilltops on a line with their eyes.

Vastey spoke: "If the French should come,
Henry, what would we do? They have not forgotten this." He moved his arm in a half circle
to include the panorama below them. "They
have not forgiven us for beating them. And
what are the reports that travelers take home?
Pétion, President in the south, Christophe, Presi-

dent in the north—two weaklings, they think.
The French, sir, have no respect for republics.
Napoleon knows that." He paused for breath.
"But if Haiti had a king!"

For an instant Vastey looked with dog-like
devotion into Christophe's face. "Majesty,
Christophe, has a ring to it! A king can order,
but a president can only suggest. The cultivators must have a master. The whole world is
watching us. They think all black men are undignified." Vastey's straight little body grew
stiff with anger. "A king—a court—a kingdom!
We would show them, sire."

Christophe's eyes sought the face of Dupuy.
He found it radiant with approbation. Henry
drew in his breath sharply and his lips drew back
from his gleaming teeth in a sudden, boyish
smile. "Come," he said abruptly. "We must
not waste time. We have a long road to go before night. While Vastey talks of kings we risk
our supper."

Dupuy and Vastey dropped behind, and as
they rode through the remainder of the afternoon
talked together in rapid undertones. Now and
then they would glance forward at Christophe.
His horse was walking, finding its way carefully
among the loose stones of the narrow trail. The

reins hung slack on its mane. But it seemed to
them that Henry Christophe rode as if on dress
parade. His long legs were thrust out and his
broad back seemed even more erect than usual.
Once he raised his right hand and set his huge
cocked hat (that was trimmed with gold braid
and bore a white ostrich plume) at a jauntier
angle on his head.

In the following month, March, 1811, the nine
members of the Council of State met privately at
a little town on the coast some distance east of
Cap Haïtien and subscribed unanimously to a
motion to make Christophe king. A messenger
brought the news to where Henry was engaged
on administrative matters in another part of the
country. The first draft of a royal constitution
had been prepared.

As he rode back to his capital the sonorous
phrases ran through and through his mind. His
big hat was tied to the saddle, his head was bare
to the blazing sun, and the wind was in his face.
The galloping hoofs of his white horse kept time.
The words tumbled under his tongue:

"President Henry Christophe is declared King
of Haiti under the name of Henry. This title,
its prerogatives and immunities, will be heredi-

tary in his family for the male and legitimate direct descendants to the exclusion of women. . . . All the acts of the Kingdom shall be published and proclaimed in the name of the King and sealed with the Royal Seal."

Peasant women ran to the doors of their mud shacks as he galloped by. His bodyguard were far behind him, outdistanced. The trees, the huts, the vistas down the valleys flashed past like the ragged vestiges of memories, but the voices of the women followed him. *"Vive le roi! Vive l'homme Christophe!"* they were calling.

Christophe, the slave, the stable-boy, the waiter, was King!

Majesty. . . . Majesty. . . . Majesty.

"Majesty has a ring to it!" Vastey had said. Christophe's head went back and a great laugh of joy came out. The wind was in his mouth. All over the kingdom the women were calling: *"Vive le roi! Vive l'homme Christophe!"*

Cap Haïtien changed its name again. It was now Cap Henry, named for the King. How Comte d'Estaing would have stared! How the young officer whose boots young Henry blacked as they sailed to Savannah would have laughed in wonder.

"Henry I." With stiff fingers and perspiring brow, while Vastey and Dupuy leaned over him, helping and guiding, he learned to write it. Henry. Once one learned it, it was easier to write than Christophe. It was shorter.

CHAPTER ELEVEN

IT WAS said that no one in Haiti slept so little or ate so fast as Christophe. The long years of campaigning had encouraged both habits. In the two months of April and May in that year of 1811 the legend of the King's haste grew to the proportions of an heroic myth. Christophe the soldier, the man of giant fearlessness, and Christophe the general, the leader who could move a regiment over the mountains with the swiftness of a parrot's flight, were well-known, well-loved figures. But administrator—that was a new facet of his brilliance. It made even his intimates blink.

Christophe kept himself closeted in the governor's mansion, now termed palace. All day, from dawn until long after the townspeople had boarded their shacks against the chill night air, members of the Council, generals and magistrates who had ridden in from the country, lounged on the broad verandah; one by one were called into the King's office, and one by one came out, their shoulders a little farther back, their eyes a little brighter; proud, and a little puzzled. The King was planning his Kingdom.

On Sunday, June 2nd, they put a golden crown on his head and a jeweled scepter in his hand.

The coronation ceremony was held in the cathedral at the Cap—a cathedral that had risen in two months from a smoke-blackened pile of stones and rotted beams on the Place d'Armes, the central square of the town. Every mason and carpenter and plasterer in the north of Haiti had assembled by royal command. They had been supplied with a company of unskilled helpers and instructed to rear the finest edifice the island had ever seen. When completed the height of the transept was 80 feet and the wall surrounded a nave that measured 250 feet on a side. There was a steeple with a place for a clock and chimes. The main altar and the lesser ones along the walls were covered with gaudy, brocaded cloth, and above them in niches stood fresh-painted plaster Virgins and Christs and saints. There was a great hole at the eastern end open to the sky, for the rich stained glass window His Majesty had ordered from abroad had not yet arrived.

A French Catholic priest officiated. His name was Corneille Brelle and his office was that of chaplain to King Henry. Christophe had proclaimed Catholicism the official religion of the state and his first act as monarch had been to build the most pretentious church ever raised in Haiti to the honor of God and Rome. What less could Père Corneille do than play his rôle with good grace—even though he knew quite well that Henry scorned his church and called his God a thing of sawdust to be dangled before the frightened eyes of slaves.

Corneille Brelle, a tall, lean, sallow Frenchman, too dry and cold a man even to sweat with natural ease beneath his cassock, was ambitious. In the name of God he invested Henry with the power and name of King.

Four princes, eight dukes, twenty-two counts,

They put a golden crown on his head and a jeweled scepter in his hand.

thirty-seven barons, and forty chevaliers attended the ceremony. They comprised the hereditary nobility of Haiti, a black aristocracy just one month old, created by royal order. Henry, who knew his people, had rewarded his friends.

That night the shabby city of Cap Henry was illumined by flaring torches and a grand banquet was given at the palace. By Christophe's special order no social distinctions of any kind were made. Gaping peasants, their black skins shining from prolonged scrubbing, danced with negro duchesses and the ladies of mulatto barons. Carpenters and artisans in starched white shirts and trousers trod barefoot on the polished boots of generals. A smattering of English and American traders mingled in elaborate good fellowship with the greatest and the least in the realm. And above them on a dais sat King Henry, garbed in a new state uniform. His legs were encased in white silk stockings and his feet were in high-heeled patent-leather pumps. A peacock-blue jacket embroidered in gold was buttoned up to his throat and tight across the upper part of his broad chest. Beneath it appeared a quilted satin vest and on his shoulders were golden epaulettes. Bonaparte himself was never appareled more beautifully or more correctly.

Every eye in the great crowd of dancers turned adoringly to his face and saw the smile that hung on his heavy mouth. The Queen, Marie-Louise, the daughter of Christophe's former owner, Coidovic the innkeeper, sat beside him. She looked at him and saw his mouth suddenly grow hard.

A new-made baron, a big black fellow who had distinguished himself in the last battle against Rochambeau, had cleared a little space in the middle of the ballroom floor and was mincing in the minuet in elaborate imitation of the Emperor Dessalines. One clumsy foot caught behind the calf of the other leg and he sprawled full length on the floor. The crowd clapped its hands and shouted with laughter, while the baron, not troubling to get up, stretched out and shouted joyfully with them. Queerly, the splendid ballroom seemed to fade away, the rich uniforms give way to rags. Before the King's mind passed an old picture—of slaves dancing by fitful firelight in the clay compound yard. The music had not stopped, but the bellow of the sweating mob almost drowned it. It was an empty, echoing, foolish sound. Christophe's hands clenched so the knuckles showed white.

"Antoine!" he called.

The baron staggered to his feet and, accompanied by the heavy breathlessness of the quickly silent crowd, reeled uncertainly to the foot of Christophe's throne. He saluted with subtle impertinence.

Christophe spoke so low the disappointed dancers could hear nothing. "Antoine, you are appointed captain of the garrison at Thomasico. You will start to-night. Perhaps you had best go now and get ready."

The baron, immediately sober, brought his right hand to his clumsy forehead in a slow salute. Thomasico, he knew, was a tiny, dirty border hamlet at the farthest limit of the kingdom. His face grew sullen. The thick eyelids dropped over his eyes. Christophe's right hand went out and grasped the baron's wrist so tight he winced with pain. "Antoine, give my regards to our friend Pétion," he said.

The baron turned and strode from the room. With confused haste the couples nearest the throne resumed their dancing.

To the queen, Christophe whispered, "Marie, so much to do and so little time." And Vastey, who stood at his left side, overheard and nodded grimly. It was plain the King had sent a volunteer to join his enemies.

·[125]·

All that week and until midnight of the following Sunday the festivities continued.

In August of the same year work was begun on King Henry's Palace of Sans Souci, and in September, 1812, it was finished.

Milot, where it was built, is a little peasant town twenty miles inland from the bay. A wide, flat valley runs between ever-lessening hills straight down to the city, so that if one climbs a bit up the slope of the precipitous, magnificent mountains that lift up just behind Milot, one commands a view of the Plaine du Nord, of the distant city, and of the harbor and the ocean beyond. It is an imperial picture in green and blue and gold, softened by the pale mists the tropic sun steams from fertile earth. There, against the hill, the King put his palace.

When completed Sans Souci was the finest mansion in the New World. It rose four storeys above the highest terrace and was built of bricks plastered over with yellow stucco. The roof was of red tile. A mountain stream was conducted under the floors of the great halls of state on the main floor to keep them cool, and the water then ran out from the keystone of a marble arch, dropped twenty feet over a bright blue wall, and rippled away through channels painted a rich Pompeian red. A grand stairway, flanked at intervals by square stone sentry boxes, led to an exceptionally large open terrace at the western end of the palace. There were banquet halls, an audience chamber, the private rooms of the King, the Queen, the young Prince Royal, and Christophe's two daughters, the Princesses Améthiste and Athénaire, besides quarters for their people. Nearby were constructed an arsenal, a royal chapel, a presbytery, special barracks for the palace guard, a storehouse, a completely equipped printing shop, a stable, a carriage-repair shop, offices, and a formal garden where the favorite fruits and flowers of Their Majesties were planted. Everything was on a scale of grandeur never before or since equaled in the West Indies.

The rooms were paved with marble and paneled with polished hardwoods. Paintings, tapestries, many mirrors, furniture, and even a fine library were brought from Europe to make Sans Souci a truly splendid monument to a black man's wealth and taste and interests.

While the building was going on and until

the last painting was hung in its proper place on the throne-room wall, Henry stayed at Milot, except when imperative business of state necessitated his riding to the Cap or over the hills to a distant town.

In a dusty uniform he directed the workmen and soldiers who were fulfilling his dream. Sometimes he would himself take a mason's trowel and work on the rising walls, remembering the trade taught him long ago when he was a slave boy on the far-away Caribbean isle.

And as he strode amid the confusion and the clatter of the building, tall young Dupuy and violent little Pompée Valentin Vastey, both barons now, kept near him and discussed the letters they would write for him.

The only contact they had with the outside world was through correspondence. Commercial and diplomatic agencies had to be established in England and the United States. Every mirror, chair, book, and tapestry had to be ordered by letter. Often in intervals of the work, while he ate and while others slept, Christophe dictated as many as a hundred epistles a day and signed each with his name.

At last Sans Souci was finished and the King and his court moved in. There were horses in the royal stable, and embossed and gilded harness, marked with the coat of arms of Haiti, hung on pegs along the whitewashed walls. A specially uniformed black regiment, called the Royal Dahomeys, was installed in the barracks.

Thursday was set aside as the day Christophe received, first commons, then nobles. Every Thursday morning at ten he took his place on a throne in a chamber done in the gilded style of Louis XIV, and held public audience. For one hour his subjects could address him directly on any matter. Barefoot, half-naked black peasants, mustachioed, dignified little magistrates, their knee-boots dusty from riding in from remote districts, negro traders and artisans, officers and private soldiers, and occasionally a proud noble of the realm came with great and little grievances and elbowed one another vigorously to have first hearings. Christophe listened to them all and passed swift judgments that were in most cases uncannily fair. As the hour drew to a close, petitions were filed to be answered the following Thursday. Then a black page boy sounded a call on a trumpet hung with blue and gold tassels. The perspiring, noisy assembly suddenly grew quiet, and Christophe would adjust his cocked hat on his head and walk from the room, his long sword swinging to his stride.

On Thursdays at five, commoners were excluded and the aristocracy of the kingdom received. On fine days the reception was held on the terrace; when rain was falling, in one of the state chambers. But, rain or shine, the nobles came.

The court etiquette was strict. Every noble was required to appear in specially prescribed uniforms that were correct and immaculate down to the last button. With their consorts they sat primly in a semicircle facing a raised dais on which were the King and Queen and their attendants. "The footstool," said the official order, "is assigned to princes and princesses and dukes and duchesses. The folding chair to counts and countesses, barons and baronesses, chevaliers and their ladies."

The position of each folding chair and its corollary noble was assigned according to rank. The highest officials of the state were near the King. Besides Vastey and Dupuy, there was the Count of Limonade and, with unconscious minstrelsy, the Duke of Marmelade. Both titles were taken from the names of important townships that had been named long before by the facetious French.

M. the Count of Limonade, by name Prévost, was an elderly and highly educated mulatto who held the important portfolios of Minister of Foreign Affairs and Secretary of State. Richard, Duke of Marmelade, was a general, and governor of the city of Cap Henry. He, too, was a mulatto. On the outskirts of the group, where formality thinned off, were men still closer to the King: Dr. Duncan Stewart of Edinburgh, Henry's physician; Mr. M. J. Moor of London, mathematician and *bon vivant;* Señor Domingo Torres of Madrid; and the Archbishop of Haiti, Jean de Dieu Gonzales, distinguished chiefly for his atheism and his supreme skill in collecting tithes. These four were white men who out of curiosity, wanderlust, and a natural yearning for profit, had gravitated to Christophe's court. They had remained because they found a certain stimulus in being close to greatness.

Dr. Stewart, a tall, dour Scotsman, and Moor, his English opposite, had become the intimates of Christophe.

They often made excuses for not appearing at the Thursday afternoon receptions, and Christophe sometimes acquiesced. But anything short of death offered by a black noble as an excuse for non-attendance, drew down upon the delin-

quent the King's furious anger—a thing Haiti
was learning to dread.

"If the French should come . . . " little Vastey was always whispering. . . . "They think all
black men are undignified."

The King on Thursday afternoons would look
with brooding loneliness into the faces of the men
and women near him. Most of them were black.
Nearly all had been born, as he had, on some
mud floor where a tired slave woman lay and
brought forth her young in lonely pain like some
wild beast. "Monsieur le Duc . . . Madame la
Comtesse," the droning voice of the Master of
Ceremonies would say—and a folding chair
would creak uncomfortably and a sooty face
would work with the strain of some stiffly phrased
reply. . . "So much to do, and so little time."

CHAPTER TWELVE

THE Thursday courts had another purpose. Plantations had been assigned by the state to all the nobles, and the King had hit upon a plan designed to make those plantations fruitful. Though most of the new negro aristocrats despised the rigid formality of the Thursday levees, they without exception adored the dignity of titles and the magnificence of their court costumes. These Christophe, who had deliberately planned cause and effect, changed at frequent intervals, and each season's official order prescribed richer materials and more costly swords and ornaments. The dukes and counts and barons, because they had no other source of income, therefore brought their lands by dint of continuous individual activity to the peak of productiveness. A tailor's bill had to be paid, and it was one thing above all others worth paying. Even negroes who could never quite break themselves of the life-long habit of sleeping on the floor, who honestly preferred boiled plantain and white rum to grouse and old champagne, agreed to that.

Under the King's strict rule the land was everywhere yielding again. By his orders, expressed in the Code Henry, every adult man and woman in the kingdom was required to work. "The following hours of labor are irrevocably extablished," read the Code. "From daylight to eight o'clock, then one hour off for breakfast on the spot; from nine to twelve, then two hours off, and from two P.M. until night fall."

The Code Henry, however, though it was rapidly making Haiti prosperous, had delicate explosive in it, especially since just over the border in Pétion's republic universal idleness was both permitted and practiced. Christophe knew this. But he had resolved to build, no matter how many bricks were cracked.

The cultivators, under the Code, were bound

to the soil. But "no landlord has authority to eject any cultivator from his habitation on pretext of illness or infirmity," it said. Hospital and medical attendance was furnished for all workers at the expense of the landlord, and no landlord, even though he was a prince of the realm or the King himself, could change his residence or fail to keep every inch of tillable soil in continuous cultivation. Landlords were required to support the "aged and infirm." They were forbidden to transfer a worker from one branch of activity to another against his wish. Soon they had bitter reason to know that cruelty or neglect of their peasants resulted in swift demotion down to the rank of common laborers.

"Slavery!" the indolent muttered. "Slavery!" shrieked the corrupt politicians in the Republic of the south. But peasants and landlords alike kept the full value of their produce, for Christophe's Kingdom quickly became self-supporting.

As the warm perpetual summers slipped by, Haiti became rich. The insatiable energy of the King put a small merchant marine afloat. His letters brought experts from England who built and equipped a weaving mill in Cap Henry which was quickly so successful that Haiti entirely ceased importing cotton cloth.

Christophe monopolized the meat supply and became the chief butcher of his kingdom. The cattle grazed on state lands and the revenue went into the state coffers. In all business deals Haiti bought with produce and sold for gold.

Christophe was himself the greatest builder and the greatest planter in his kingdom. Sans Souci before long was one of seven only slightly less gorgeous royal palaces. Besides these, as time advanced, he erected fifteen châteaux. Each was in a different part of the kingdom and each was surrounded by wide and fertile lands that were continuously planted and continuously reaped.

From the leaded windows of Henry's bed-chamber at Sans Souci he could see several of his smaller mansions in the midst of mile upon mile of rustling cane fields. In one year his plantations had produced 10,000,000 pounds of sugar, two-thirds of the kingdom's total export of that commodity. Under the stimulus of the work laws the port of Cap Henry alone had, in a single year, besides sugar, exported 20,000,000 pounds of coffee, 5,000,000 pounds of cacao, 4,000,000 of cotton, and a quantity of logwood, fruit, and other minor country products.

England was in a radiant mood at being the

handler of such magnificent trade and she triply enjoyed it because it profoundly irritated the French. Out of gratitude, she made Christophe the fashion.

Clarkson and Wilberforce, just then busied in bringing England to declare for the universal abolition of black slavery, entered into correspondence with Christophe, gave him much useless advice, and quoted his career as a proof of what negroes could attain to. More and more Englishmen came to settle in Haiti. A handsome clubhouse for their use was built from the shell of an old plantation manse outside of Cap Henry at the limit of the coastal strip beyond which no Europeans were permitted to go without special permission of the King. And the Foreign Office, moved by overwhelming curiosity, suggested that Sir Home Riggs Popham, commander-in-chief of the West Indian fleet, call at Haiti and then write his impressions.

Sir Home Popham's fleet had rested in the harbor of Cap Henry several times. The Cap lay on the way to Jamaica, where the Admiral made his base. It was a convenient shelter during the hurricane months, and an occasional visit of full-rigged men-of-war put heart in the Britons who bought coffee beans and sold Birming-

ham iron pots in the whitewashed stores in
Henry's still half-ruined capital.

The sailors from the ships frequently came
ashore. On one particular night certain seamen
felt they had had enough of the meager adven-
tures the port afforded, and at about ten o'clock,
their elbows interlocked for support, they reeled
down to a shore-front jetty where their boat was
moored. One carried a bulging burlap sack. A
negro sentry, almost invisible in the pale starlight, stood on the pier. He challenged the Englishmen and told them they must show him the
contents of the sack. Nothing, he explained,
could leave the port without customs inspection,
and in the absence of proper officials he, the sentry, was the customs.

With thoroughness and nautical emphasis the
sailors cursed him for a damned black bastard and
explained that as seamen of His Majesty they
could go and come as they pleased, taking any
number of burlap sacks with them. The sentry,
who understood as little English as they did
Creole, remonstrated, so they knocked him neatly
off the end of the jetty into the dirty shallows of
the bay. A crowd of negroes appeared out of
the shadows and in another moment a young Brit-

ish officer who happened by had drawn his sword and was challenging the world.

King Henry was in the city that night at a ball. A messenger who was sent for him explained that the quarrel was rapidly spreading to the proportion of a riot and begged the King to come. Christophe, who was wearing a uniform of white satin trimmed with gold, hurried down to the beach.

The crowd of negroes fell back silent, leaving the now partly sobered Englishmen standing in a defiant group. The black monarch walked close to them. They were men of average size, but Christophe towered above them. They realized with scorn they were in the presence of the "nigger" King, but they likewise realized they were in the presence of a man who, though middle-aged, could readily take any three of them and crack their fuddled heads together.

The enraged and dripping sentry explained. Before he was done the English officer, a young lieutenant, gave an angry order to his men and started down the jetty steps to the boat. Christophe reached out and took him by the slack of his coat just under the chin and lifted him ignominiously off the ground. Then, with the Briton's apoplectic and startled face a few inches from his own, he said to him in a tone of aggravating calm: "My soldier is right. The laws of the port forbid taking goods off without examination. But in obeying the letter he forgot that drunken children will not likely have anything of value. Go back to your ship, and if we have no further trouble I will not report you to your superior."

With a slow smile and an uncomfortably sudden jerk Christophe let the officer's kicking feet touch the earth. He turned about, and as he walked away through the darkness he found it wise not to hear the curses which the white men, now safe a few yards offshore in their rowboat, bellowed after him.

The story was carried to Sir Home Popham. The next morning he asked for an official audience at Sans Souci.

A painted royal carriage drawn by four gray horses came down to the port for him, and with courteous young Dupuy as escort he was driven for two hours along the wide, stone-paved royal road that ran straight from the gate of Cap Henry to the palace. With growing wonder and admiration Sir Home listened to Dupuy's informed talk of politics and books and personalities, and watched the panorama of cultivated fields run by on either side. And at the end of the drive Dupuy conducted him up the grand staircase to where King Henry, surrounded by the high officials of the court, awaited him on the terrace.

The Admiral, a tall, distinguished Englishman, wore his full-dress uniform, but he found himself eclipsed by the splendor of Henry and his courtiers. Painfully he realized that the afternoon was hot and his broadcloth more appropriate to the bleak chambers of Windsor than to the verdant terraces of Sans Souci. Had he not been a gentleman, Sir Home would have been very uncomfortable indeed.

Christophe stepped forward, shook hands, and greeted him with courtly propriety. Sir Home had turned the matter over and over in his mind without reaching a decision, but the phrase he had debated came naturally to his lips. "I am honored, Your Majesty," he said, and bowed.

Dupuy introduced Sir Home Popham to the others. With a sense of increasing ease he shook hands with Count Prévost, with Vastey, with Duke Richard of Marmelade, and with Moor and Dr. Stewart. Then they all went into the library and tea was served.

It was the first official visit Christophe had

received from a foreign power, and he had given elaborate orders pertaining to the formalities which were to be observed. It was vital that England, Haiti's best customer and most valued friend, be impressed through her envoy. But that night, after a state banquet at which Sir Home drank vintage champagne from golden goblets and wiped his lips with a damask napkin embroidered with the coat of arms of Haiti, he found himself on a moonlit balcony outside a lighted window, leaning his chair against the palace wall. Unconsciously he unbuttoned his tight jacket at the collar. Christophe was at his left and near them were seated Dupuy and Moor and Dr. Stewart.

For some time Moor and Stewart and Christophe had made it a custom to sit together each evening at the same place on the terrace. The two white men would take turn about reading to their king, their chairs tilted back against the palace wall so that the light from the window fell on the pages in their hands. Moor was an amateur specialist in world politics. The leading journals and the official documents of England and France came to him and it was his duty to go carefully through them and read aloud the more important and relevant passages. Christophe, his black forehead wrinkled with attention, used to interrupt when words and references cropped up which he did not understand, and both friends would explain. Dr. Stewart performed a similar service in the realm of literature. The best books, essays, verse, and fiction, published currently in London and Paris came under his scholarly eyes, and he read the things he judged best to the King—who fought against ten thousand years to understand.

"Your Majesty," said the Admiral, "if you will pardon my saying so, that was uncommonly fine duck."

Christophe, in the shadows, answered, "It is a special cross I have bred for the table, part common duck and part Muscovy. I shall send a brace to your ship tomorrow."

Dr. Stewart chuckled. "Henry, Sir Home, finds time for everything."

They sat there until the lights in the windows of Sans Souci went out one by one and the full moon rose high into the iron blue dome of night.

Sir Home had recently visited Port au Prince

and talked with Pétion. Henry pumped him for detailed news.

The republic, thanks to Pétion's corrupt officials and his worthless tin currency, was close on bankruptcy, it seemed, but Sir Home insisted that its strength was not to be underestimated.

"Your work laws," he told Christophe, "are unwise. In the south they say your subjects are no better than slaves and that you are a second Dessalines. You are going too fast. Pétion has an army and if you ever stumble he will be over the border and at you, and every man and woman in Haiti who confuses idleness and independence will join him. . . . Sorry. I don't know why I fancy I am privileged to advise you." The Admiral coughed apologetically.

For a long moment Christophe was silent. The others peered at him intently through the half dark. When he spoke his full rich voice seemed suddenly old.

"You do not understand. . . . " He stopped again, seemed to be struggling for words. Then he went on:

"My race is as old as yours. In Africa, they tell me, there are as many blacks as there are white men in Europe. In Saint Domingue, before we drove the French out, there were a hundred negroes to every master. But we were your slaves. Except in Haiti, nowhere in the world have we resisted you. We have suffered, we have grown dull, and, like cattle under a whip, we have obeyed. Why? Because, m'sieu, we have no pride! And we have no pride because we have nothing to remember. Listen!" He lifted his hand.

From somewhere behind them was coming a faint sound of drumming, a monotonous, weird melody that seemed to be born of the heart of the dark, rearing hills, that rose and fell and ran in pallid echoes under the moon.

The King went on. "It is a drum, Sir Home. Somewhere my people are dancing. It is almost all we have. The drum, laughter, love for one another, and our share of courage. But we have nothing white men can understand. You despise our dreams and kill the snakes and break the little sticks you think are our gods. Perhaps if we had something we could show you, if we had something we could show ourselves, you would respect us and we might respect ourselves.

"If we had even the names of our great men! If we could lay our hands"—he thrust his out—

"on things we've made, monuments and towers and palaces, we might find our strength, gentlemen. While I live I shall try to build that pride we need, and build in terms white men as well as black can understand! I am thinking of the future, m'sieu, not of now. I will teach pride if my teaching breaks every back in my kingdom!"

His voice at the last had risen to a subdued roar of passion. When he had done, he stood up so suddenly his chair clattered noisily on the stone flags. He strode away from them down the terrace and went out of their sight through a doorway into his palace.

In a few minutes Dupuy retired. The three Englishmen—the Admiral, the physician, and the mathematician—sat talking until the sky grew gray with the approach of dawn.

Early the next afternoon King Henry invited Sir Home Popham to witness a review of his household troops. A rich carpet was laid on the main terrace under the shade of a tall star-apple tree. Chairs were arranged, and the King, the Queen, the Admiral and numerous mulatto and

negro officials took their places. At a nod from
Henry a bugler blew a call and from around a
wall at the left came a company of soldiers,
marching eight abreast.

The Admiral gasped. Every man in the procession was at least six feet tall, all were full-
blooded negroes, they wore elaborate and splendid uniforms, and they marched, the trained eyes
of the Englishman noted, with a marvelous precision. Their polished muskets were all at the
same angle, and every booted foot swung in time.
Each company wheeled, presented arms, and
after it passed the reviewing place disappeared
from view down the grand stairway.

As each regiment appeared Sir Home was
treated to the spectacle of a different but hardly
less striking uniform.

The afternoon advanced, but the endless, un-
broken procession still continued. Sir Home
Popham, dazed and marveling, estimated that
not less than 30,000 men had passed before them.

At twilight the King asked the Admiral if he
had seen enough, and Sir Home wearily assented.
Christophe gave an order and the last file of men
marched down the stairs.

As they went indoors, Christophe asked the
Admiral if Pétion could boast any such display of

men, and Sir Home, with vigorous emphasis, shook his head.

He did not know that an important detail of the review had been concealed from him—that as each squad passed from sight the men broke ranks, turned off when halfway down the grand stairway, and filing through a concealed opening in the wall, hurried by an underground passage to the barracks behind Sans Souci, and that there they changed their uniforms and fell into ranks to pass in new guise before the throne again. Christophe had taken advantage of the European notion that all negroes look alike and had treated him to thirty views of the same one thousand men.

CHAPTER THIRTEEN

IN CHRISTOPHE'S time English educators were much concerned with the "modern" teaching theories of Joseph Lancaster, and the British and Foreign School Society with headquarters on Borough Road, London, had been established for the purpose of carrying out that once famous gentleman's theories.

Christophe heard of the society, corresponded with it, and before long drove down to Cap Henry to greet six Lancastrian teachers who had come to Haiti at his urgent invitation. By special proclamation the six Englishmen were declared exempt from the passport and other restrictions which to some extent limited the free movement of other white men in Haiti. And before they had wholly recovered from their seasickness, Henry placed gangs of masons and carpenters at their disposal and told them to build schools.

In a miraculously short time exact replicas of their far-away structure on the Borough Road, London, were erected in the four principal ports of the kingdom—Cap Henry, and Port de Paix on the north coast, and Gonaïves and St. Marc on the west. And, so Henry could watch the work, one was built at Milot just under Sans Souci.

Educated mulatto and negro men were found, put through a swift course of instruction, and installed. Soon the five national schools were giving instruction to over two thousand pupils.

The study of English was required. The more advanced students were urged to learn Spanish. Two-thirds of the island was owned by Spain and the King dreamed of a greater kingdom. Christophe, who had never learned to read or write, was ambitious for the future of the blacks.

It was his own fancy to found a royal college. Out of his own purse he established a chair of anatomy and surgery and arranged for Dr. Stew-

art, who was already director of the royal hospital, as well as private physician to the King,
to give occasional lectures. In Pétion's republic
educated men flatly refused to turn their energies to anything more productive or less dignified
than government clerkships—a peculiarly mulatto tendency. So black Christophe compelled
every boy of ten years old or more to learn a
trade. He supplied the masters and the tools.

Ever since the peace which followed the expulsion of Rochambeau, Baron Vastey had been the
tutor of King Henry's only son, fat, domineering,
obstinate Prince Victor-Henry.   For years
Madame Christophe had devoted several hours
every day to the task of instructing their two
daughters, Améthiste and Athénaire. But the
education of Marie-Louise, though great for the
wife of a negro waiter, was inadequate for the
consort of a King and she soon came to the end
of her knowledge.

Sometime, when a little more was done and the
friends of the negro were a trifle more numerous
and more generous, Henry hoped the princesses

might go abroad. So it was important they be taught all graces and accomplishments. He began to cast about for special tutors for them.

Dupuy said Philadelphia was a center of propriety and culture and suggested that through friends there he could probably find teachers in every way suitable for the position. Christophe intrusted the business to him.

After a prolonged correspondence two Americans were selected, and after natural delays arrived at Cap Henry. They were two white maiden ladies well past middle years.

History has neglected to preserve their names, unique though they were in the annals of feminine adventurers. But tradition has it that one was tall and lean and virulently correct, and the other, her life-long friend, rather plump and jolly, and that they wore tight-waisted black spencers and knitted mittens without fingers. It is also recorded that their voyage from Philadelphia lasted fifteen days and was stormy all the way, with the result that they arrived at the Cap very pale and much depressed in spirit.

Baron Vastey met them. As the two gallant Philadelphians alighted from the small boat which brought them from their ship's place of anchorage, he offered an arm, and in the same instant, with his eyes like twin points of fire, asked the startling question:

"Ladies, what would you do if the French should come?"

To that, with great presence of mind, the taller one replied: "Sir, we would place ourselves under the protection of His Majesty King Henry," and Vastey was silent.

The city of the Cap was a bitter disappointment. It was rising newborn from the ruins, but ruins there still were. And the clatter and confusion of the building which was everywhere going on was hardly more cheering than the piles of old embers. Cap Henry was so little, the ladies confided to each other, hardly more than a village. It boasted almost no cultured society. Baron Vastey was very learned, of course, and the English schoolmasters were of one's own sort . . . but it was hard not to be a trifle homesick.

With careful courtesy they indicated to Baron Vastey that it might be pleasanter if room could be found for them at the palace. The original plan had been that they were to live in Cap Henry and drive each day out to Sans Souci.

King Henry readily assented. But five weeks passed before the chambers at the palace were ready to receive them. At the end of that time Baron Dupuy drove in for them.

A cool breeze was blowing in from the sea. There were flowers at each side of the road and the negroes at work in the fields were singing. Dupuy asked them many questions about Philadelphia. The ladies gradually relaxed into a new cheerfulness.

On their arrival under the mounting, splendid walls of Sans Souci, a more superb structure than the Americans had ever seen before in all their lives, a pleasant middle-aged mulatto woman whom Dupuy introduced as the Duchess of Port-Margot, wife of the King's nephew, greeted them with informal courtesy and showed them into a grand *salon* filled with people—the full court.

Many of the younger negro nobles had never seen a white woman before. One exclaimed aloud upon their beauty—which was pleasant but a trifle upsetting.

At eleven, after coffee and time to refresh themselves after their journey, the ladies were shown into the library and in a moment six black pages in gold and blue livery entered, followed by King Henry.

They had had no idea he was so tall. Nor had they imagined him as quite so "dark complex-

ioned." But his large eyes were kind and smiling
and his gracious manner put them at their ease at
once. He asked them to be seated; but "of
course," they later confided to friends in Philadelphia, "we refused."

Before nightfall the two ladies had met the
Queen and discovered her to be a gentle and
kindly mistress. They had talked with the princesses, found them "congenial," and, what impressed them most of all, they had learned from
Henry himself that he had played an humble part
in the American War of the Revolution. Christophe, who loved to reminisce, had roused that
first adventure for them from the storehouse of
his faded memories and had painted a vivid
picture.

"It makes one," remarked the stout little
maiden lady to her friend, "feel quite at home."
And she smiled with intrepid reassurance.

Before long the two ladies found things remi-
niscent of Philadelphia singularly precious.
Athénaire and Améthiste were willing and cheer-
ful pupils. The Queen, when she was not se-
cluded in her beloved garden, was kind. Mr.
Moor and Dr. Stewart were most agreeable, of
course. But, when all was said and done, life at
the palace of Sans Souci was, frankly, dull.

Milot, in spite of its being the residence of the sovereign, was only a tiny negro village half asleep under the tropic sun. Each day was the double of all others.

The court, following the lead of the King, who rarely devoted more than five hours of the twenty-four to sleep, rose early, but only Christophe seemed able or willing to keep every moment of the long, murmurous hours of daylight filled with some sort of activity.

Nearly every morning His Majesty might be seen striding down the grand staircase across the lower park and disappearing into the concealing jungle that clothed the mountains that rose up on three sides of the palace.

It was his invariable custom to take a daily walk, accompanied by a page who carried his battered brass telescope wrapped in a white napkin. No one knew just where he might go, but every cultivator, landlord, and civil servant within a radius of fifteen miles knew that Christophe might appear at his elbow any moment. Then woe betide anyone whom he found idle! Much was going on and he gave his personal attention to everything. Roads were being made, bridges built, reservoirs constructed, farms surveyed, and a postal service to every section of the kingdom being organized. The telescope played an important part in each undertaking. From rocky eminences in the hills the King would look down into the near-by valleys. Often peasants would be punished because from a distance he had sighted them asleep in the sun during the hours the law set apart for labor. The brass telescope, the uses of which were only vaguely understood, soon gave the King a reputation for magical omnipresence.

But what troubled the ladies from Philadelphia, at first subtly, then acutely, was a mood which they sensed was gathering slowly over the majestic peace of Sans Souci.

There were whispers in the corridors and queer looks exchanged. On several occasions they could not help observing that conversations between courtiers broke off suddenly and that voices shifted to an artificial note on their approach. It made them nervous. The King seemed so pleasant and so "capable." They wondered if it were possible he had enemies. Obviously something was seriously the matter. Perhaps, they confided to each other, it was the Citadel.

In 1819 the Citadel had become the supreme absorption of the King. The ladies from Philadelphia had never visited it. Due to the formation of the hills, it was invisible from Sans Souci, but in the five weeks they spent at Cap Henry they had often noted its immense gray silhouette on the summit of the cone-like mountain the peasants called Le Bonnet à l'Evêque, and its history was common talk.

The Citadel la Ferrière, was the gigantic fortress King Christophe was building on the crown of a peculiarly inaccessible mountain 3,000 feet above sea-level. Work on it had been begun in January, 1804, at the order of Dessalines, and for fifteen years the work had gone toward completion. But not until Henry had been King for seven years, not until Haiti had been made immaculate, her fields planted and her people enriched, had the King driven on the work with more than common urgency.

Its construction was a task to stagger the ambition of a Pharaoh and to test the utmost skill of the engineers of any time. But the Citadel was to answer many purposes. It was to be a refuge against that dreaded but receding time when the terror of Vastey might be fulfilled and the jealous French would come. It was to be a great gray fist thrust threateningly into the sky to warn the yellow men beyond the border that majesty was not to be trifled with. But above everything, it was to be the king's grand gesture, a dream of empire wrought in everlasting stone, a monument the blacks could turn their eyes to, lay their hands on, the essence and the foundation of their pride.

A Haitian mulatto engineer named Henri Besse had evolved the design under Christophe's supervision. Following the original specifications, the fortress took the shape of an irregular square, tapering to a gigantic prow that pointed magnetic north. The height of the walls, measured from the tip of the steeply sloping mountain-crest, ranged from 80 to 130 feet. They were from 20 to 30 feet thick and surrounded a central parade ground.

As the work progressed the original plans were elaborated. In spite of the difficulties of the situation—the Citadel was at the end of a strenuous three hours' climb up a winding and sometimes dangerous trail—365 huge bronze cannon, one for every day in the year, were dragged up and ranked in batteries. And hundreds of casks of gunpowder, thousands of fifty-six-, thirty-, and twelve-pound iron cannon balls were borne up the trail by panting, sweating men and women and piled in chambers behind the guns.

An enormous underground cistern caught every drop of rain that fell on the Citadel. A miniature palace for the King was erected at one corner of the parade ground, and another, somewhat larger, named after the King's favorite bird, *Le Ramier,* was constructed at some little distance on a neighboring hill-slope. There were deep dungeons, treasure chambers, powder magazines, long corridors of cannon, and room sufficient in an emergency for the housing of a garrison of 10,000 men. La Ferrière, as Christophe proudly knew, was more gigantic than any fortress ever erected on this side of the sea.

But it was costly. While the fear of France had been close, the work, carried on chiefly by soldiers of the standing army, had gone forward with little protest. But by 1819 Haiti had grown fat from prosperity and France at last seemed far away.

In 1814 Louis XVIII had sent two envoys to Haiti to negotiate for a return of the island to the status of a French colony. But Henry had executed one of them as a spy and sent the other ignominiously home with a jug filled with tiny seeds and instructions to tell Louis that twice as many men as the jug held seeds would be required for Haiti's subjugation.

In 1815, on Napoleon's return from Elba, he had written King Christophe suggesting an alliance between them. Henry had replied with a short contemptuous challenge.

Why then, grumbled the nobles, must Henry still have his Citadel? They hated it. It took money that might have found its way into private pockets and men who could have swollen retinues. Besides . . . somehow, without a word being spoken or a law proclaimed, it had become Henry's own, not theirs or Haiti's. It was, they knew in their hearts, magnificent—the supreme physical creation in the history of the negro race —but it was *his*. He had dreamed it and his vitality had got it done. And Henry, the rich, the educated, and the powerful could not forget, was a full-blooded black.

That was the rallying call, that the foundation fact on which was being reared a growing discontent.

CHAPTER FOURTEEN

WHEN Christophe became chief governor in 1807 the mulattoes, who filled the upper stratum of Haitian society, had expected him to grant them special favors. Many claimed large tracts of plantation land as their hereditary property—hereditary because the mulattoes making the claim were the bastard children and grandchildren of the Frenchmen who had formerly held the land. Henry had been so ungracious as to laugh at them. That had reopened an old wound.

After his last military expedition against Port

au Prince, he had returned to discover that in his absence the leading mulatto women of the Cap had held a special service in a church to pray to the Virgin for his defeat and death. On that occasion Henry had not seen fit to be amused. In a fury he had sent soldiers into the city at night to find and kill the women most conspicuous in the treason.

After he became king, tranquillity still eluded him. Scarcely a month had passed without the discovery of some plot against him somewhere in the kingdom, and without exception mulattoes were most deeply concerned. So far, the King had always found them out and always meted vigorous punishment, either death by the sword of Gaffie, the black executioner—who was so skilful he claimed he could take a head off without soiling the adjacent collar—or hard labor on the ever-mounting walls of the Citadel.

Once the French priest, Corneille Brelle, discovered a highly organized and widespread conspiracy among secret adherents of Pétion who lived in the Kingdom. They hoped to murder the King and hand the country over to the Republic. For that the conspirators were executed.

On another occasion some rich young mulatto men formed a poetry club at Cap Henry and called it *Le Petit Vers*—a seemingly innocent enough business. But it happened that in the King's garden grew a special kind of coffee tree whose berries, known at Sans Souci as *Les Petits Verts,* were reserved for the royal table. Christophe suspected a mocking pun and the poets were sent to work on the fortress walls. The educated Haitians had always found vast amusement in an ex-slave's pretensions to Epicureanism.

After less than half a year in Haiti the two ladies from Philadelphia went home. "We take with us only the pleasantest recollections," they said, and courtsied to the King. He himself drove them down to Cap Henry and saw them off.

Christophe had gone too fast, and because his people did not share his ambition and his energy he grew savagely impatient. Soon no one felt safe from his furies.

Duke Richard, governor of Cap Henry, and chief aide-de-camp of the King's military household, was a man of great authority in Haiti. No one below the King had a more devoted personal following among the soldiery than he. But once Christophe found him sprawled asleep in the grand *salon* at Sans Souci and noted that his uniform was wrinkled and disarranged. He took Duke Richard by the throat and shook him as a terrior shakes a rat. No one must let down. The work was not yet finished. Pride, dignity— these had become obsessions of the King.

Soon afterward Henry learned that Richard had again relaxed. He had again been careless and again shown indolence, this time in carrying out an important matter of state business. For that Henry sent him to work for three months on the walls of the Citadel in company with common criminals.

Once Christophe, standing on the walls of the Citadel, looked through his telescope and saw a negro farmer more than a mile away in a valley far below him, lying sound asleep by the door of his mud-walled cottage. The King knew the man. Twice before he had reprimanded him for idling during the stipulated hours for work. His lips drew back from his teeth in a snarl of sudden.

senseless rage. He called for a captain of artillery and together they went into the cool, long gallery where the huge bronze cannon were ranged behind their little windows in the wall. The young captain, obedient but trembling, took aim, while Christophe grunted with the labor of dragging on the ropes that turned the heavy gun carriage. It was ready loaded. Henry lit the fuse and the morning quiet was shattered with the reverberant, resounding roar of the explosion. But the man asleep in the sun did not hear. The hurtling cannon ball, superbly aimed, smashed him and his mud hut together.

There was no doubt that he had changed. His enemies said that he was drunk at last and dangerous with too much power. Even his friends wondered if now that more than half the century of life was behind he had not, with weariness and age, slipped back into sullen savagery, a stain that perhaps old ugly Africa had put on him.

Sir Home Popham, the English Admiral, had come often to Sans Souci. In the summer of 1820 he came to say good-by. His health had broken and he was going home to England. They were both old—or so they thought themselves—and perhaps they would not meet again.

In the heat and silence of a week-day afternoon they climbed the hill together. The boy with the telescope followed at a distance. They found a shaded rock from which one commanded a view of the Plaine du Nord and the white houses of Cap Henry twenty miles away. The lean, distinguished British sailor and the giant negro sovereign sat down and mopped the perspiration from their foreheads. For a few moments they were silent. The King's huge frame was curiously relaxed. He had grown heavier lately and little furrows ran out from the corners of his eyes.

"They tell me, Henry," said the Admiral at last, "that you have turned tyrant. Why?"

Christophe's hands opened in a queer gesture of helplessness. His head bent down and for a moment he looked unseeing out toward the far-away sea. He spoke with measured, dull precision.

"Maybe I know no other way. Sometimes a fury comes over me and there is a foul taste in my mouth. I am blind with anger. . . . Last night I learned that my chaplain Corneille

Brelle was in correspondence with men in the south. Why? I don't know. Perhaps because he could never tame me for his church. More likely because I would not compel the peasants in the hills to kill their snakes, their poor little gods, or break their drums. Brelle calls them damned. . . . His reasons do not matter. Letters were found under his cassock, and that is enough. He has already told them in Port au Prince how many soldiers I have and how many guns. He will lose his head at dawn to-morrow. That is what you call tyranny?"

He drew in his breath sibilantly and his voice took on more volume and a new richness.

"I know no other way. No man hates waste more than I do. I am angry if I see red coffee berries rotting neglected on a tree. The lives of men are precious, too. Each time I must condemn a man to die it wrenches me, perhaps a little more, perhaps a little less. . . . But, Sir Home, though I am King, though they call me Majesty, you must remember I am still an ignorant old man. I cannot read. What other men have thought and done is no help to me, except what I learn of them through my friends. . . . When I took an army to Port au Prince after they had killed Dessalines, I frightened them so badly I lost half my kingdom. 'Christophe,' they say, 'is stupid. All he understands is war and work. All he wants is a fortress and power. He is no politician.' Perhaps all that is true. But in the time that remains to me I must do what I wish as I will. I have many enemies, I know. There is not a plot against me I don't know of. Some of the fine fellows down there," he pointed to the red roof of Sans Souci below them, "would be frightened if they knew how much I know! But do you see these?"

Two great clenched fists were thrust out and his eyes sought the Admiral's face. "My courtiers tell me I am king because of my brains, because I know so much. That is nonsense! I am king because of these! So long as they are strong I will have a thousand friends to every enemy. Even my friends don't love me, but if they obey me that is enough. When death opens this fist the work will be done. Haiti will be great, strong, rich, proud—so proud it will last forever! Then the blacks will not forget the name of Christophe."

The King rose to his feet and held his hands out before him in a strange ecstasy. His eyes were bright, and his lips stiff with the intensity of his mood.

"Come now, if you are rested. I have a commission which I would be obliged if you would fulfill for me in London."

That night Sir Home Popham took aboard his flagship a heavy iron chest sealed with the royal seal. It contained $6,000,000 in gold to be deposited in the Bank of England in the name of Marie-Louise Christophe.

At dawn Gaffie, the executioner, struck off the head of the French priest, Corneille Brelle. He died pronouncing a curse on the name Christophe.

Henry was absent all that day from Sans Souci. In the late afternoon, as had become his invariable habit, he climbed the steep trail that led to the fortress on the mountain peak. Once there he granted only a curt nod to the officers of the Citadel garrison and went into his private chamber. A sentry outside the door heard the clicking of billiard balls. A table had been carried up the mountain, a task that took many men days, and was installed in a high-domed room that gave on a wide terrace from which one commanded a view of a third of the kingdom. When Christophe was a waiter he had marked the shots of French planters who lounged at the Crown Hotel. When he became King, billiards was his favorite diversion. Usually he played with officers and courtiers, but this afternoon he played alone.

After a little, as the twilight mists were scudding up from the sea and breaking softly against the great prow of the fortress, he came out dressed in a dusty ragged coat, torn knee breeches and a pair of battered boots.

The workmen were just coming down from the walls. He took a mason's trowel from a black prisoner and mounted a ladder to a point on the highest rampart.

The soldiers of the garrison, the prisoners, and the conscript peasant laborers ate their evening rice and plantains around little fires in the parade ground. That night they talked in whispers and kept their eyes turned up to where the lonely figure of their King was silhouetted, a tiny mark against the luminous night sky. The regular click-slap, click-slap of his trowel throwing mor-

tar and tapping the big flat bricks came faintly
down to them. Often in recent months he had
worked at his old trade of mason on the walls of
La Ferrière. Several times he had worked till
daybreak and boasted that he, unaided, had done
as much in a night as they had accomplished in a
day.

The peasants whispered that on these lonely
vigils he buried golden treasure.

In the great sections of the walls he raised
there was ample room, they reasoned, for banded
iron chests containing millions upon millions of
American and English coins. . . . It was common knowledge that in the great vaults under
the lowest dungeons there was a national treasure
in gold that amounted to approximately $30,-
000,000. And, it was argued, if Henry could
collect that much for the purpose of purchasing
the San Domingan section of the island from
Spain—a deal that was in an advanced stage
of negotiation—how much, then, would he not be
apt to set aside for himself?

In the hundred years the Citadel's been empty,
many men have gouged great holes in its massive
walls seeking for what Christophe hid. But their
failure to find anything lends credence to the
claim advanced then by Henry's friends—that

he labored on the walls for the selfsame reason
that he bullied Duke Richard and sent so many
to their death—because he was fired with a giant
impatience; because in the year 1820 the King
was ridden by a sense of haste that tortured him.

CHAPTER FIFTEEN

THREE hours after sundown that night he flung his trowel down, retired to his room again, and changed into his customary ornate uniform. Then, with a few parting directions to the mulatto engineers in charge of the construction, he let himself out of the studded oaken door that gave on the lower terrace and in a few moments the sentries on the walls saw him far below them, striding down the moonlit trail toward Sans Souci.

What the King did in that single day became a legend. To climb to the Citadel, to work there, and then to come down the narrow, dangerous path in the dark to the palace again would consume the last shreds of most men's energy.

But, at midnight, Christophe knocked softly on a bedchamber door. In a moment a sleepy head appeared, followed instantly by the night-shirted figure of a middle-aged negro baron, a former general in the army of Dessalines who had been promoted by Christophe to the post of military general of the Citadel.

The baron, startled and frightened, saluted. Over his shoulder appeared the worried black face of his wife. She held a lighted candle high over her head. Henry nodded reassuringly. "It is nothing, madame. But, Baron, I have an errand for you. I will wait here while you put on some clothes."

The baron disappeared into the room, while his lady wavered in the doorway, uncertain as to whether it were better to leave the King unceremoniously in the dark, or, still more unceremoniously appear before her sovereign barefoot in her nightgown.

Christophe met the situation by closing the door.

In a few minutes the wondering baron joined him in the shadowy corridor.

It was three o'clock in the morning when the old soldier returned to his chamber. The baroness, her gnarled negro hands clenched in nervous fear, sat on the edge of their bed, the candle guttering on a table beside her. With a whispered greeting her husband stepped into the narrow circle of light. The woman leaped to her feet with a scream.

"My God! Raymond, you are wearing Henry's uniform. You have killed the King!"

"Sssh. Be quiet. You'll wake the palace. Nothing is the matter. Christophe is going to be abroad all night and he fears assassins. He changed clothes with me in case . . . you see? He is wearing my uniform." Then he told her of his errand.

"Henry and I have buried some treasure behind the Queen's garden. The chest was too heavy for even the King to carry alone. I helped him. It is for Marie-Louise, he told me, but he said she doesn't know anything of it herself. He made me swear on my life I'd keep the secret until a time came when she might need money. Henry is a good husband. . . . Mon Dieu, but I'm sleepy! Let's go to bed. . . ."

Soon only the tall sentries in their boxes on

the grand staircase were awake—and Christophe, who was walking somewhere restlessly in the wooded mountains, his hands clasped tight behind his back and his agile mind tumbling troubled through a maze of hopes, ambitions, fears.

The following day Henry gave orders that his meals were to be served to him alone in his private apartments. The solitary, brooding mood of yesterday still was on him. He ate ravenously.

At one o'clock he gave orders to a body-servant to saddle a horse. He was going to the village of Limonade, ten miles away, to attend mass.

The servant gaped stupidly. Never before in anyone's memory had Henry gone to mass. Certainly not alone. State ceremonials, yes. . . . Recovering himself, the man hurried to the stables.

It was the hour when most of Haiti was indoors asleep. The vertical rays of the sun pounded more and more relentlessly on one's back with every mile down the dusty, empty road. But Henry rode without mercy, whipping his

sweating white horse to a gallop that soon outdistanced the men of his bodyguard.

The Church of St. Ann, patroness of maiden
ladies, is a simple oblong building with a peaked
roof. The interior is drab and shadowy, the
staring, painted saints along the walls rather
lonely, vacuous figures. It had rarely been visited by communicants more eminent than barefoot, still hopeful old negresses who came to pray
to kind St. Ann.

The fat Breton priest who lived nearby was
asleep in the hammock when a breathless soldier
roused him with the news that King Henry was
awaiting him in the empty church.

In a moment he was in the little anteroom that
adjoins the sanctuary. A frightened peek
through the door assured him that Christophe,
whose great body, tilted head, and outstretched
hands seemed to fill the meager space by the
altar, was waiting. The King was kneeling at
a little praying-stand.

With trembling hands the priest put on his
vestments. In a minute he was ready. But so
furious had been his haste that it occurred to him
that not a gust of breath was left in him. De-
cidedly he was in no state to give Communion

to the King. He paused in the doorway to recover himself. From where he stood he could
see Christophe, but Christophe could not see
him. Suddenly the fat priest's mouth dropped
open and his little blue eyes nearly started from
his head.

Christophe was slowly rising to his feet. His
left hand clutched the *prie dieu* so tightly the
wood cracked noisily. His right arm, rigid as
an iron rod, was thrust out. His fingers pointed
at the altar. He had turned a little so the priest
could see his face. It was gray beneath the
brown. Little flecks of white foam were showing
at the corners of his mouth. His eyes were staring horribly. Now he was standing erect, a black
giant in a queerly incongruous bright blue uniform. Frozen helpless with fright, the priest
realized Christophe was about to speak. His lips
moved helplessly, then words were formed.

"Great God! it's Corneille Brelle!"

The King had seen the ghost of his dead chaplain officiating in strange silence before the altar.
With a scream he crashed forward. In the fraction of a second before panic gave wings to the
priest's heels he saw that the blow against the
stone floor had laid Christophe's head open. As

he fled, he realized that the fallen King was lying limp in an ever-widening red puddle.

Two hours later, Dr. Duncan Stewart, the frightened Queen, Vastey, and Dupuy were at Christophe's bedside in the priest's house. The men of his bodyguard had carried him there.

While the tall, frigidly calm Scotch doctor stripped the unconscious monarch preparatory to making his examination, Vastey, consumed with impatience, ran out into the midst of the gaping, silent crowd of peasants that had assembled. In a shrill, high voice he ordered that every goat, every burro, and every dog within a radius of three miles from Limonade be taken at once by its owner outside of the district; that every mother of a young child depart at once, not to return to her village until permission came. There must not be a single sound anywhere that might disturb the King. Vastey gave rapid orders to some soldiers. Men were to be stationed at every road and trail that led into Limonade, to prevent curiosity-seekers from coming too close. Then, quite forgetting his dignity, little Vastey ran back to the priest's house.

As he tiptoed into the whitewashed room where his old friend lay, Dr. Stewart was saying to the Queen, "A stroke. Apoplexy induced by extreme fatigue and apparently some mental shock. He will recover, but there may be complete paralysis. . . ." Then, startlingly, the Scotchman added, "Oh, good God!"

For two days Christophe lay unconscious, while not a sound broke the summer quiet of Limonade. On the third day the Queen and Stewart, who had sat by him in a ceaseless vigil, saw his eyelids flutter open and a look of gray, ghastly terror cross his face. Then he saw them bending over him and smiled. That evening he was carried in a special litter to Sans Souci.

The news ran over Haiti. The voices of black farmers carried it, calling from hillside to valley, over across the ranges, across the deserts, the great central plain, and at last into the dry brown hills of the south. At night the rumbling drums of old witch-men sounded the refrain, colored it, dramatized it weirdly and sent the word in code over the marshes where the night birds called and across the narrow strips of sea to lonely little islands off the coast.

Christophe, lying in magnificence in the vast and splendid palace under the hill, heard, when night lay breathless on his kingdom, and his hands caught at his silken sheets. "So much to do." Then, weakly, he fell asleep.

The next morning young Dupuy and Dr. Stewart came into the King's chamber. The leaded windows were open on a brilliant sky and a cool breeze from the sea fluttered the hangings. One could hear the King's horses whinnying in the stables four hundred yards away.

Christophe was awake and hungry. His face was radiant with cheerfulness. But Stewart had directed him to be perfectly still and he meekly obeyed.

Dupuy and Stewart seemed strangely ill at ease. He laughed at them. Stewart was always saying he had a perfect constitution. With stiff awkwardness Dr. Stewart took his place on one side of the bed and Dupuy on the other.

"Come, Henry, let's get up," said the Scotchman, and held out his hand.

Christophe's arms lifted to them. He put his hands in theirs, raised his head a little . . . and cursed softly. With a force that nearly tumbled the two men over him, he pulled at their arms. Slowly his great body came out from under the

·[182]·

covers. His nightshirt, open at the throat, exposed his broad black chest. His head turned toward Stewart, and his eyes, wide and frightened, sought the Doctor's.

"Duncan, what's the matter? I can't move."

They let go his hands. Stewart flung back the bedclothes, and while Dupuy, his pale brown hands knotted desperately together, looked on, he went methodically over the limp body of the King.

At last: "You might as well know, Henry. Except for your head, your arms, and those hands of yours—and God only knows why he spared those—you are paralyzed. Know what that means?"

Christophe nodded.

That night the hidden drums and the sing-song, wailing voices of the peasants carried fresh, exciting news.

In Port au Prince the mulatto politicians heard and rejoiced. Pale, indolent Duke Richard in his mansion at Cap Henry remembered how Christophe had made him work on the fortress walls with common criminals. His thin lips twisted in a smile. Mulatto chevaliers and barons of the Kingdom stroked their chins reflectively. Henry, who despised all vanities of color, had forbidden his aristocrats to grow beards. He knew what pride men with a little white blood in their veins took in whiskers. He had laughed at them. . . . But now, perhaps . . .

Thick-lipped, dull-eyed blacks in the hot sweat of the cane fields spat on the ground and wondered. They arched their backs, yawned, then laughed. It would be good to rest. *Sacré!* There was too much sugar.

And in St. Marc, the city of the kingdom that lay nearest the border of the republic, two officers of the garrison excused their regiment from duty for a week and entertained at their table officers of the army of the Republic.

But the King, in spite of his infirmity, had rarely been more active. Four of the strongest, tallest black soldiers of his household regiment were attached to his person. On fine days they carried him to a balcony that adjoined the top-floor rooms of the palace. There, with his telescope beside him, he could see the richest region of his kingdom spread out like a pale green carpet below him. All day long messengers would ride

·[184]·

up the royal road to bring him reports, petitions, papers.

Vastey, Count Limonade, and Dupuy were always within call.

Word came of the treason of the officers at St. Marc. Christophe called a negro general to him, a man named Jean Claude, and instructed him to take a company of faithful men to the rebellious city. The two officers and all others, both military and civilian, who had been bitten by revolution, he said, were to be brought to him in chains, so he himself could have the relish of trying them and condemning the guilty. The King's hands pounded furiously on the arms of his throne. They must know their sovereign was master still.

But Jean Claude never reached St. Marc. He was shot through the throat that night less than ten leagues from the palace. He and his men had fallen into an ambush prepared by a company of revolutionists. They had come under cover of the thick forests that clothed the most inaccessible parts of the hills to feel out the sentiment of their countrymen in the north. Messengers took the head of Jean Claude in a sack to Port au Prince as a kind of symbol to friends

in the republic of the "good faith" of the St.
Marc garrison.

A frightened peasant came at dawn to the
gates of Sans Souci. He had a message for the
King, he told the sentry. He was at once admitted and fell prone by Christophe's chair.

The man was panting from exhaustion and
whimpering with fear, but his message was
definite.

The soldiers from St. Marc had left their con-
cealment. They were marching on the public
roads and as they marched they were shouting
for all to hear: *"A bas le Roi! Vive l'indépendance!"* And, more particularly, they were prom-
ising no more work, free rum, and spoils to all
who joined them. A few peasants, not many,
had already joyously thrown down their machetes
and were in the procession. They were moving,
very slowly, it was true, toward Sans Souci. And
no one was resisting them.

Christophe's hands caught the chair arms and
with a great effort he lifted himself up, but he
sank back groaning. His eyes stared terribly
while two servants lifted and pushed him to the
natural position in his chair, but no sound came
from him. The kingdom was toppling about his
head and the King was more helpless than a new-

born calf. Timorously, his eyes sought the massive hands lying on his lap, and for an instant a grim smile wiped the heavy tragedy from his mouth.

"Vastey," he shouted, "send a horseman to Cap Henry. I have a message for Duke Richard. He is to report to me here at once."

Baron Vastey's mobile little hands sprang forward in a gesture of protest. His mouth opened. Then his eyes found Christophe's and he saluted smartly and turned away.

Richard, Duke of Marmelade, presented himself on the King's balcony five hours later. A blue silk canopy had been spread to protect the King from the full force of the noon sun. October is the month of heaviest rainfall in the north of Haiti and the air was thick with moisture.

Richard wore his smartest court uniform. But the perspiration, for all his nervous mopping with a handkerchief, ran in little streams down his temples. His distinguished, aquiline face twitched with complex emotions as he faced Christophe.

For a moment they looked intently at each other, then the King, in a quiet voice, said: "Richard, I wondered if you'd come. I am flattered that you are still afraid of me. . . . You have heard the news, of course. The St. Marc troops have passed Ennery on their way here. You have my orders to take the Cap Henry garrison and march against them."

Richard's right hand lifted to his forehead in a leisurely salute, and for the fraction of a second a smirk played across his face.

Christophe's head thrust forward and he reached his left hand out. The movement, so strangely dissociated from the deathlike stillness of his paralyzed body, was somehow terrible. Richard paled.

"And before you go, damn your dirty yellow soul, you may get on your knees and kiss your master's hand!"

For an instant there was utter silence on the balcony, except for the quick breathing of Baron Vastey, who stood by Christophe's chair. Richard's lips grew white with anger.

Then, as if an invisible hand were pushing him down, he dropped slowly to his knees, leaned forward, and put his lips to Henry's outstretched heavy hand. Then he rose, saluted swiftly, and went away.

Christophe said to Vastey, in a choking voice he strove to make seem natural:

"It is a sound principle of warfare, Pompée,

to concentrate all the enemy's forces in one place. By midnight that traitorous swine will have taken all his men to join the St. Marc troops. We have no time to lose. Send word that I will review the army to-morrow morning at ten o'clock."

CHAPTER SIXTEEN

AMONG the under servants at Sans Souci was an old black man, born in Africa, who professed to be a witch doctor. He had first come to Milot in chains to be tried by the King for the offense of practicing his trade without proper regard for the Kingdom's laws "governing the medical profession." But Christophe had acquitted him and he had stayed on at the palace.

At daybreak this man was brought to the King's bedchamber.

For two hours the witch doctor, aided by a

valet, massaged Henry's body with a mixture of
red pepper and raw rum, a liniment held in great
esteem in the old slave days. At nine o'clock
they dressed him in his most splendid blue-and-
white-and-gold uniform and at ten his four bodyguards propped him in a throne-like chair and
carried him down the stairs and out on to the
main terrace at the palace's western end.

Below, filling the narrow valley of Milot and
stretching away into the humid distance, were
the assembled regiments of the army of Haiti,
their rich and vivid uniforms glinting brightly in
the morning sun. Certain companies were miss-
ing, but it was a lack no one spoke of.

Every eye was turned toward the palace. Half
the army saw the King's chair being carried to its
place on the terrace. Five thousand blacks could
hear Christophe's booming, roaring voice break
the silence:

"Bring me my horse," he called.

It was the first sound he had uttered that day.

The white horse, fully caparisoned, was waiting behind a wall. In a complete and breathless
quiet a groom led it across the terrace toward
Henry's throne.

At sight of it a vast shouting smashed the
silence. With a single voice the army cheered,

"Vive le Roi! Vive l'homme Christophe!" Down the valley thousands of hats were flung into the air. The hoarse, gigantic shouting beat against the mountains and rolled back in thundering echoes. Drummers in the ranks pounded wildly, fiercely, on their drums.

The horse came to a stand ten feet from the throne. The four bodyguards turned toward the King. He shook his head and swept them away with his arm. He twitched off the robe that covered his lap.

Dr. Stewart, standing in the crowd, pulled at his clean-shaven chin and stared.

Christophe looked straight before him. He breathed deep. The cheering suddenly ceased while the echoes faded down the valley. Christophe stood erect.

In five powerful, headlong strides he reached the white horse. One hand went to its mane, the other to the saddle. He bent a little to leap up. But while the court and army looked on, King Christophe slowly, slowly, like an empty bag, slumped down till he lay under the horse's feet with his arms outstretched and his face against the earth. The strength so miraculously summoned for the instant had gone out of him.

Rain had fallen during the night. When

*While the court and army looked on, King
Christophe slowly, slowly, like an empty bag,
slumped down till he lay under the horse's feet.*

Stewart, the Queen, little Vastey, and Dupuy picked him up, his uniform was smeared with mud. Dry sobs were shaking him.

When they set him back in the throne the soldiers below cheered again, but this time the sound was scattered and half-hearted. The Queen bit her lips. The gaping courtiers near by noted with astonishment that sour, silent Dr. Stewart, was smiling with a queer proud smile and that tears ran unashamed down his furrowed cheeks.

The King gave an order. A page ran down the stairs to where the first company of soldiers stood by the singing fountain that fell over the bright blue wall.

The parade began.

As each platoon passed the throne where Christophe sat the men broke into spontaneous cheers: *"Vive le Roi! Vive l'homme Christophe!"*

A little beyond him a clerk sat at a table and gave each man as he passed a gift from the King of four *gourdes* of money.

Then, because they had reached the far end of the west terrace, the line of marching men turned around a high garden wall that hid Christophe from their sight.

The review lasted several hours. Christophe sat upright and kept his right hand rigidly in salute. But when a third of the procession had passed him, two sorts of cheering sounded faintly in the valley.

As the soldiers passed before him they called, *"Vive l'homme Christophe"*; as they passed around the corner of the wall out of sight of him, they broke ranks, and, all unconscious of the contrast, shouted, *"A bas le Roi! Vive l'indépendance!"*

Each company had been touched by the revolution. Duke Richard and the generals associated with him had given word that there was to be no more work, that the Kingdom would become part of the Republic, and that all men at last were to be gloriously free. "The tyranny is ended," was the cry.

They had come to the review drawn by a lingering dread and a lingering love for their King. But the master had crumpled into the mud, and though, when his eyes were on them, they cheered and stayed in stiff parade, once out of his sight they were quit of him.

At last the tail of the procession, still meek but not cheering, passed and Christophe turned his head to find that the nobles, the generals, the servants, the gentlemen and ladies in waiting who had stood behind his throne in the morning, had quietly slipped away. Except for a few who stood close to him he was alone.

The valet and the witch doctor; elderly, wise Prévost, Count of Limonade and Secretary of State; Dupuy; Baron Vastey; three old, erect black generals; the Scotch physician; the fat Prince Royal Victor-Henry; the young negro princesses, Athénaire and Améthiste; and Marie-Louise, his beloved, gentle, simple Queen, were there beside him. A stone's-throw away was the palace of Sans Souci—queerly named—its doorways empty and its leaded windows swinging wide. Evidently the last of its servants and sentries had gone away.

The King lifted his hands helplessly to them and they carried him through the echoing, silent palace up to his balcony.

They brought him his battered brass telescope. He sent one of the generals down the royal road to find out the progress of the rebellion and bring the report back.

Athénaire and Améthiste, his daughters, one twenty and the other twenty-two, sat on the ground and laid their cheeks against his knees. He sent the others away.

He saw the solitary general, who somewhere had found a rich, brocaded banner, ride proudly

down the wide white road toward Cap Henry.
The old man went as if a great army followed
close behind him. Two hours later, in the twilight, he came back. A rebel sniper had shot off
his cocked hat and he had lost his banner. He
was still alone.

Christophe sent his daughters away and asked
for Dr. Stewart. The sun sank below the far-
away rim of the sea and the night rode swiftly
up the hills. Soon the valley of Milot was dark
and murmurous. The sunlight touched the
mountain peaks and then was gone.

The Scotch doctor sat on a stiff chair beside
the King. They had been friends so long, talk
was superfluous.

Once Henry whispered: "Toussaint, the Tiger,
and I. . . . We dreamt so much and we have
done so little."

Again, with a certain rich pride in his tone, he
said: "To be great, Duncan, is to be lonely. To
be magnificent is to have men hate you."

The sky was red with the reflection of flames.
The King's châteaux in the Plaine du Nord were

on fire. Through the brass telescope one could see little dancing shadows pass before the pyres of flames. Now and then an isolated shot, a sound of distant cheering, and a brief mad rumble on a tom-tom drum came up to them. Christophe cleared his throat.

"Duncan, they will be here soon now. You must go. There are still horses in the stables, I think. Take whatever you can find that's worth anything, then go by back trails to the Cap. You will be safe with the English consul. . . . Good-by."

"Henry," said Dr. Stewart, "don't be a God-damned fool."

He stood up. "I am going to send Marie-Louise and the children to you, but I will be over the hall if you want me."

They shook hands.

The Queen and the King's three children came to him. He then sent for Vastey and Dupuy. He said good-by to them all, gave, in something of his old tone of command, orders that the two men were to take his family at once to Cap Henry and put them under the protection of English friends there. He gave Marie-Louise the papers that entitled her to the fortune Sir Home Popham had deposited in the Bank of

England for her. Then he kissed them and sent them away.

When they had gone he called his valet and asked him to bring a bowl of water.

While the man stood by he slowly washed his hands and dried them on a damask napkin. Then he sent the man away.

But the servant stayed outside the door of the King's bedchamber and watched through the keyhole.

He saw Christophe, after a long, quiet minute, throw himself off his chair and with clutching fingers drag himself across the room to a closet. He saw him reach up and turn the knob, saw him pull down a snow-white satin gown, roll himself into it, and then, like some stricken animal, drag himself horribly across the floor to his bed and lift himself on to it.

From where he lay Christophe could look down the valley. It was not empty now. It was filled with a shouting, running mob of men carrying torches.

The King took something from a little cabinet by his bedside. While the trembling valet still peered hypnotized through the keyhole watching him, he fell back and lay still. A tall clock in the corridor ticked regularly.

Running feet sounded on the stairways. The first of the looting rebels were already in the palace.

A great crash of broken glass was heard.

"They are breaking even the mirrors that have imaged me!" said the King aloud, and his voice was broken.

He clenched his right fist and raised his left hand, which held a pistol, to his temple.

A shot reverberated, followed by sudden quiet. The King was dead. He had put a golden bullet, molded long ago, through his brain.

Marie-Louise and the others had disobeyed the King's command. They gave gold and jewels to the looters to bribe them not to mutilate his body. They tied sheets to two poles, laid Christophe on the improvised stretcher, and at midnight the Queen, the two Princesses, and little, fierce old Vastey left Sans Souci by a secret door and started up the long, dark trail that leads to Henry's Citadel.

The dead King was a heavy load; doubly heavy

for one old man, an old negress, and two young girls, all heartbroken.

But all that night they labored up the trail, while Stewart and Dupuy and the three generals rode with Prince Victor toward Cap Henry.

Dawn found the cortege on the last half mile of the winding trail that snakes over bare ground just under the gray walls of the fortress. As the night mists rose and broke against the prow the sentries on the wall saw them. No news had come to them up there. The sudden shout resounded, *"Le Roi est mort!"* The sentries left their posts, the laborers and soldiers who were forming lines for the morning parade took up the shout, ran down the corridors behind the cannon, and burst out the lower door.

A handful of officers and men tried vainly to stem the tide. But when the Queen and Vastey with their burden ended the climb and came under the portals of the fortress door the Citadel was empty and the hillsides were alive with running, laughing men on their way to join the rebels in the valley.

Slowly, panting and weak from exhaustion, they staggered through the galleries and came out in the sudden brightness of the central court.

The morning was cool. Green parrots flew caw-
ing overhead.

The few faithful soldiers and officers who had
stayed behind came to attention. Willing hands
reached out and took the heavy stretcher.

Vastey and the governor of the Citadel entered
into a quick whispered consultation. *"There was
no time."*

The Queen and the Princesses must be rushed
to safety.

A pit of new mixed builders' lime lay open in
the center of the parade ground. Vastey and
the governor lifted the stretcher high over their
heads and with a tremendous effort turned it over.

The King's body pitched from its winding
sheet, turned in the air, and with a sullen splash
fell into the lime. It sank down and the white
corrosive lipped in on it like a hungry mouth.
The bystanders caught their breaths. The surface of the lime was still and smooth. But above
it, through it, thrust up the King's right hand
and his bare black wrist. The hand was clenched.
It seemed in death to be still masterful, still
strong.

"There was no time." They left him there.

In the empty, gigantic fortress on the moun-

tain-top the King's hand threatened the stillness
and the morning sky.

The revolutionists, fearful lest the royal line
go on, murdered Prince Victor-Henry. They let
Marie-Louise and the daughters go away.
Améthiste died eleven years later, and her sister
lived for eight years after her. Marie-Louise,
the Queen, outlived her lover and her King by
more than thirty years. They had found comfort in religion and all are buried in a little cemetery behind the monastery of the Capuchins in
Pisa, Italy.

But Christophe's kingdom scarce outlived the
night. The republic closed the schools and let
the farms fall to weeds and rank jungle. His
palaces stayed empty.

But for nearly twenty years the three black
generals guarded Henry's Citadel. The old men
took turn about and did sentry-go upon the walls.
They built a little stone hut over the lime pit and
in the vacant fortress that on sultry days stands
in gray, gigantic loneliness above the clouds that

fill the valleys, they dreamed and found comfort in their memories.

For a while the peasants called the days that followed his fall, *"Le temps de notre malheur,"* and for two generations they paid him the tribute of a careless term. They forgot the title King. No one called him Majesty, or Henry, or Christophe. But till the last of the people of his time had gone away they spoke of him, when tired thoughts turned back to the old years, as, simply, *"L'Homme."*

The Man.

The pride he had hoped for—just a little, in that word they called him by, long after he was dead:

Christophe—L'Homme.

THE END

BIBLIOGRAPHY

(Arranged in order of the importance of their bearing on the subject of this book.)

HARVEY, W. W.—*Sketches of Hayti from the Expulsion of the French to the Death of Christophe.* London, 1827.

MADIOU, THOMAS—*Histoire d'Haiti.* 3 vols. 2nd edition. Port au Prince, 1922.

LÉGER, J. N.—*Haiti, Her History and Detractors.* New York, 1907.

BROWN, J.—*The History and Present Condition of St. Domingo.* Philadelphia, 1837.

BASKET, SIR JAMES—*History of the Island of St. Domingo.* London, 1818.

RAINSFORD, MARCUS—An Historical Account of the Black Empire of Haiti, London, 1805.

MALO, CHARLES—*Histoire d'Haiti,* Paris, 1825.

FIRMIN, A.—*M. Roosevelt et La République d'Haiti.* New York, 1905.

SANNON, PAULEÚS—*La Guerre de L'Indépendance.* Port au Prince, 1925.

DORSAINVIL, DR. J. C.—*Manuel d'Histoire d'Haiti.* Port au Prince, 1926.

MACKENZIE, CHARLES—*Notes on Haiti.* 2 vols. London, 1830.

SANDERS, PRINCE—*Haytian Papers*—with a Preface by the Compiler. London, 1816.

Black Majesty

BELLEGARDE, WINDSOR—*Petite Histoire d'Haiti*. Port au Prince, 1921.

CANDLER, JOHN—*Brief Notices of Haiti*. London, 1842.

OSTERHOUT, MAJOR G. H.—"A Little-known Monument of the Western Hemisphere"—Article in *National Geographic Magazine*. Dec., 1920, U. S. A.

NILES, BLAIR—*Black Haiti*. New York, 1926.

Almanach Royal d'Hayti—Pour l'année 1818 (& 1820). Présenté au Roi par Buon. À Sans Souci, de l'Imprimerie Royale.

VALENTIN, POMPÉE, BARON DE VASTEY—*Essai sur les Causes de la Révolution et des Guerres Civiles d'Hayti*. À Sans Souci, de L'Imprimerie Royale, 1819.

VALENTIN, POMPÉE, BARON DE VASTEY—*La Système Colonial Dévoilé*. Au Cap Henry, Octobre, 1814.

VALENTIN, POMPÉE, BARON DE VASTEY—Réflexions sur les Noirs et Les Blancs. Au Cap Henry, Mars, 1816.

VALENTIN, POMPÉE, BARON DE VASTEY—Réflexions Politiques sur Quelques Ouvrages et Journaux Français concernant Hayti. À Sans Souci, 1817.

PRÉVOST, COMTE DE LIMONADE—*Relations des Glorieux Evénments, etc.,* Cap Henry, 1811.

DE LACROIX, COMTE PAMPHILE—*Mémoires pour Servir à l'Histoire de la Révolution de Saint Domingue*. 2 vols. Paris, 1820.

NEMOURS, COLONEL—*Histoire Militaire de la Guerre d'Indépendance de Saint Domingue*. Paris, 1925.

Procès Verbal Des Séances du Conseil Général de la Nation, Oct. 21, 1814. Au Cap Henry.

Précis Historique des Negociations entre La France et Saint Domingue, Paris, 1826.

Black Majesty

STEPHEN, JAMES—*The History of Toussaint L'Ouverture*. A new edition with a Dedication to His Imperial Majesty, the Emperor of All the Russias. London, 1814.

STEPHEN, JAMES—*The Opportunity, or Reasons for an Immediate Alliance with Saint Domingue*, London, 1804.

MOSSELL, REV. C. W.—*Toussaint L'Ouverture, The Hero of Saint Domingo*. Lockport, New York, 1896.

BEARD, REV. JOHN R.—*Life of Toussaint L'Ouverture*. London, 1853.

MARTINEAU, HARRIET—*The Man and the Hour*. New York, 1873.

BENJAMIN, R. C. O.—*The Life of Toussaint L'Ouverture*. Los Angeles, 1888.

GRAHAM, HARRY—*Splendid Failures ps. 42-78*. London, 1913.

FRANKLIN, JAMES—*The Present State of Hayti*. London, 1828.

HANNA, REV. S. W.—*Notes of a Visit to Some Parts of Haiti*. London, 1836.

MAGLOIRE, AUGUST—*Histoire d'Haiti 1804-1909*. Port au Prince, 1909.

DE ROSIERS, COMTE—*Hayti Reconnaissante*. Au Sans Souci, 1819.

BIRD, M. B.—*The Black Man—or Haytian Independence*. New York, 1869.

CHALMERS, COLONEL—*Brief Remarks on the Late War in St. Domingo*. London, 1802.

Communications received at the Foreign Office Relative to Haiti, London, 1829.

DE LAUJON, A.—*Souvenirs de Trente Années de Voyages à Saint Domingue*. 2 vols. Paris, 1835.

Black Majesty

JANVIER, LOUIS JOSEPH—*Les Constitutions d'Haiti 1801-1885.* Paris, 1886.

HAZARD, SAMUEL—*Santo Domingo, Past and Present—with a Glance at Hayti.* New York, 1873.

GRÉGOIRE, A.—*De la Liberté de Conscience et de Culle à Haiti,* Paris, 1824.

PRICHARD, HASKETH—*Where Black Rules White.* London, 1900.

REDPATH, JAMES—*A Guide to Hayti,* Boston, 1860.

STODDARD, T. LOTHROP—*The French Revolution in San Domingo.* Boston, 1914.

MARCELIN, FREDERIC—*Choses Haitiennes.* Paris, 1896.

FRANCK, HARRY A.—*Roaming Through the West Indies.* New York, 1920.

CANCELADA, DON JUAN LOPEZ—*Vida de J. J. Desalines, Gefe de los Negros de Santo Domingo.* Mexico, 1806.

JOHN W. VANDERCOOK

JOHN W. VANDERCOOK, although still in his early twenties, has already gained fame as a travel writer and as an anthropologist. While a young newspaperman out West, he witnessed the lynching of a Negro, and that awoke his interest in the whole Negro problem. He has been to every Negro republic on the face of the globe. With his young wife, a well-known sculptor, he spent many months in Haiti and the Dominican Republic, studying psychological and political conditions, and gathering material for his biography of the Black Emperor—Henry Christophe—whose story he has told so vividly in *Black Majesty*.

His first book, *Tom-Tom*, was written as result of a visit to Suriname in South America, when he went into the jungle and lived with the natives, studying their extraordinary civilization.

SEE NEXT PAGE

TOM·TOM

TOM-TOM, Vandercook's first book, aroused unusual interest not only in the literary world, but among those interested in primitive peoples and primitive psychology.

Arthur E. Spingarn, noted Professor of Philosophy at Columbia University, wrote to the author: "*Tom-Tom* is written in the spirit of Rousseau and Chateaubriand, but the Negro has a right to such idealization as much as the Indian. It is a fascinating and enlightening book and deserves a great success. My slight acquaintance with the Guianas made it all the more real to me."

The strange world so vividly evoked in *Tom-Tom* lies deep in the treacherous jungles of Suriname, on the north coast of South America. Its inhabitants are bush Negroes, a remarkable and almost unknown people descended from African slaves brought to Suriname nearly two hundred years ago. "In the great jungle," writes Mr. Vandercook, "they have builded a society, a philosophy, a science, and an art which belongs in the jungle and enables them to live there, to triumph over the disasters of material misfortune, and attune their hearts and minds to the weird mood of the forest. . . ." Mr. Vandercook tells the story of that civilization and the valiant struggle that made it possible. He has captured the wonder of jungle life; he has written with sympathy and comprehension of the devious and fascinating psychology of the remarkable bush Negroes and the extraordinary things they have accomplished. There is a haunting beauty in *Tom-Tom* with its graphic descriptions of the great forests and the lives of those who live there.